T H E   B O O K   O F

TAPAS
AND SPANISH COOKING

THE BOOK OF

TAPAS
AND SPANISH COOKING

HILAIRE WALDEN

Photographed by
JON STEWART

PUBLISHED BY
SALAMANDER BOOKS LIMITED
LONDON

Published 1993 by Salamander Books Limited
129-137 York Way, London N7 9LG, United Kingdom

© Salamander Books Ltd 1993

ISBN 0 86101 653 X

Managing Editor: Felicity Jackson
Art Director: Roger Daniels
Photographer: Jon Stewart, assisted by Sandra Lambell and Nicole Mai
Home Economists: Kerenza Harries and Jo Craig
Typeset by: BMD Graphics, Hemel Hempstead
Colour separation by: Scantrans Pte. Ltd, Singapore
Printed in Spain by Bookprint, S.L.

ACKNOWLEDGEMENTS

The Publishers would like to thank the following for their
help and advice:
Barbara Stewart at Prop Exchange, Unit F,
51 Calthorpe Street, London WC1.

Notes:
All spoon measurements are equal.
1 teaspoon = 5 ml spoon
1 tablespoon = 15 ml spoon.

CONTENTS

INTRODUCTION

The Spanish cuisine is one of the most exciting, rewarding and varied in the world as it encompasses dishes that contain a kaleidescope of ingredients, prepared in myriad styles to suit perfectly every occasion, taste and diet. *The Book of Tapas and Spanish Cooking* brings you the best examples of all these styles. There are simple dishes flavoured with herbs, vibrantly-coloured and richly flavoured meat and poultry casseroles with equally tasty vegetable versions, as well as light, quickly cooked ones, and dishes based on rice and dried beans that are ideal one-pot meals, plus warming, hearty soups contrasted by those that are the epitome of summer eating.

There are all manner of fish recipes to serve for sophisticated eating or family suppers, with eggs for snacks and plenty of cakes and pastries to satisfy those with a sweet tooth.

The Spanish cuisine is essentially a family one, developed out of the ingenious exploitation of accessible local raw materials, and the imaginative and best use of foods that were readily available.

Based on simple ingredients, with its roots firmly in home cooking and pure country food, Spanish cooking is essentially hearty and unpretentious; ingredients are inexpensive, flavours direct, recipes easy and presentation straightforward with no unnecessary show. The criteria for the success of a dish is whether it tastes good.

In line with the trend that exists in respect to other national cuisines such as French and Italian, people, both Spaniards and foreigners, are now taking a closer look at 'traditional' Spanish food, increasing its reputation and expanding awareness of it. There is a growing band of 'new wave' chefs who are researching old dishes, refining them to suit modern tastes, and making Spanish food fashionable.

SPANISH COOKING

True, traditional Spanish cooking is many faceted. Indigenous foods and traditional culinary practices have been reinforced throughout the country's long history by the absorption of new ingredients and cultural influences from many different countries. The Romans left their imprint, principally in the irrigation of parts of the east coast, and the introduction of olives; while 700 years of Moorish occupation resulted in almonds, citrus fruits and fragrant spices becoming integral ingredients in Spanish cooking. The discovery of the New World resulted in the introduction, and wide acceptance, of tomatoes, sweet and chilli peppers (capsicums), courgettes (zucchini), many types of beans, potatoes, chocolate and vanilla.

Furthermore, Spain covers areas as diverse as sparse mountain ranges, arid plains, fertile orchards and arable lands, olive and fruit groves, regions that are cold and wet, and those that are hot and dry, coasts facing two different seas – the Mediterranean and the Atlantic – and many rivers. Not surprisingly, each different area yields different foods and calls for a different type of cooking.

However, there are a number of ingredients and flavours that distinguish Spanish food. The olive is vital, particularly for its oil; Spain is the greatest consumer of olive oil in the world. Garlic is an indispensable element in the majority of dishes. Parsley is the popular herb, and nuts appear frequently, often ground to make a sauce. Onions, green and red peppers (capsicums) and tomatoes are the other constants.

FOOD OF THE REGIONS
The Basque province has both wonderful fish and seafood from the Atlantic ocean and some of the finest cattle, sheep and dairy foods in Spain. Portions are large, as is to be expected in a cold climate, but the cooking has a certain refinement. Dishes cooked *al chilindrón*, in a flavourful sauce based on the particularly good local red peppers (capsicums), and tomatoes, onions and garlic, are typical of Navarra and Aragon. Trout from the clear mountain streams that rise in the Pyrenees are a regional favourite, especially cooked with ham.

The food of Catalonia is exciting and richly varied and features interesting sauces, such as Romesco (see page 114) and Allioli (see page 34), aromatic herbs and noticeable similarities with French Mediterranean food, such as Zarzuela (see page 62), a close cousin of bouillabaise.

Valencia and Murcia form one of the most densely populated and richest agricultural areas of Europe, and exhibit distinct Moorish influences. Here there are groves of oranges and almonds, large market gardens and rice fields. The last two provide the ingredients for authentic Paella Valenciana – the addition of fish and shellfish is a modern adaptation that has become universally popular. Andalucía is the land of olives, olive oil and sizzling fried foods, particularly the varied sea and shellfish from around the long coastline. In contrast, Extremadura is a land of tough, hardy countrymen, and simple hearty cooking with many stew-type dishes.

The vast, exposed Central Plain produces Spain's most well-known cheese, Manchego (see page 9), as well as many other sheeps' milk cheeses. The area is most generally thought of as a land of roasts, principally young lamb and suckling pigs.

Galicia and Asturias are renowned for the quality of the fish and shellfish, and as the home of excellent Empanadas (see page 24). The climate is comparatively cold and wet, so appetites tend to be hearty and the local dishes correspondingly warming and filling. Locally-produced cider is popular both for drinking and also for using in cooking.

EATING PATTERNS
The traditional breakfast is usually eaten in cafés and consists of churros with large cups of hot chocolate in which the churros are dunked. Coffee and sweet cakes or a light snack are eaten at mid-morning. Lunch, the main meal of the day, is at 2 o'clock, but is often preceded by tapas, usually taken at a bar or café on the way home or to a restaurant. Work is returned to in the late afternoon. About 6 o'clock is the time for a *merienda*, light snack, with tapas being eaten from about 8 until 10 o'clock, when it is time for dinner. This is usually lighter than lunch.

TAPAS

Originally, and still in some bars today, tapas were simply a few olives or almonds, and perhaps a selection of cheeses, sausages and serrano ham and possibly cubes of tortilla served, often free, to accompany a glass of fino sherry. But nowadays, tapas have come to encompass more or less any hot or cold dish that can be served in small portions, and they may be quite substantial. They are displayed along the lenth of the counter of a bar or café to be ordered in a group, or individually.

Although quintessentially Spanish, tapas are so well-suited to today's style of casual eating, that they have caught the popular imagination outside Spain. A selection of tapas is ideal for an interesting informal meal, and they are wonderful fare for a party, buffet, picnic or barbecue. Most can be made quickly and easily, a great many can be made in advance and served at room temperature while others can be partly prepared and then finished at the last minute before serving.

INGREDIENTS

Cheese: Although Spain produces about 200 cheeses, only Manchego enjoys any degree of reknown, and is the only one exported in quantity. Manchego may be mild and quite soft, or strong and hard. It is made from sheeps milk, so is quite expensive. If Manchego is not available, use freshly cut Parmesan cheese.

Chillies: These play an important role in Spanish cooking, adding not only heat but distinct flavour to dishes. Different varieties of chillies impart different flavours and degree of heat. Generally, large chillies are milder than small ones, whilst dried ones are often hotter than fresh. Red chillies are ripened green chillies, and so they have a sweeter, more rounded flavour compared to the fresher, 'green' taste of the immature form. Avoid touching your eyes or any cuts, and always wash hands thoroughly afterwards. If you have sensitive skin, wear rubber gloves when handling chillies.

Chorizo: The best chorizo contains as much as 95% pork. Other ingredients are pork fat, salt, garlic and paprika, which gives it the pronounced red colour. The most widely known and available chorizos are fully cured and can be eaten without cooking, for example, as a tapas or in salads. There are two degrees of spiciness, picante (hot) and dulce (mild).

The other type of chorizo, which has to be cooked, is found in stews and in bean and potato dishes, which will be coloured red by the leeching out of the paprika in the chorizo. These chorizos are short and stubby and come linked together in the same way as English sausages. They sometimes have added flavour from being smoked over oak fires. Oregano is also sometimes added.

For the best and truest flavour use good Spanish chorizo, but if unavailable use paprika sausages, which are usually found in Italian delicatessens.

Garlic: This is essential in Spanish cooking. Use the freshest possible – if there is any sign of a green shoot in the centre of a clove, remove it as it imparts a bitter taste to a dish. Buy garlic bulbs that are plump and firm and store them in a cool, dry place. Raw garlic has a pungent flavour, but when it is cooked, the taste mellows to give a subtle background flavour, and whole cloves can be eaten. Chopping garlic gives a more pronounced flavour than crushing it.

Herbs: Parsley is an important herb in Spanish cooking. The flat-leaved, Continental type is used. Oregano makes an occasional appearance, while bay leaves and thyme are quite widely used, especially in dishes which require long cooking. The presence of mint, most popularly with broad beans and chicken, is a legacy left by the Moors. Fresh herbs give a better flavour then dried ones. However, if you do have to use dried herbs, reduce the amount in the recipes by a half to two thirds.

Ham: The most well known Spanish ham is *jamón serrano*. This is a raw, air dried ham and is often eaten in thin, though not wafer thin, slices carved along the grain as a tapa. The best *jamón serrano* comes from the black Iberian pig, but the supply is limited. *Jamón serrano* is also used for cooking, when it is more thickly sliced so it can be chopped into chunks. Italian prosciutto is the nearest substitute.

Olive oil: Olive oil lends a characteristic flavour to many dishes. For general cooking, use a pure Spanish olive oil as it has a mild flavour, and keep the more distinctly flavoured, and more expensive, virgin oils for dressings. Keep olive oil in a cool, dark place, but not the refrigerator, and use within a year.

Onions: Yellow Spanish onions have a sweet and mild taste.

Paprika: *Pimentón dulce*, produced from ground dried red peppers, is an essential element in Spanish cooking, adding a characteristic flavour and colour to many dishes. It is added at the beginning of the cooking and is fried to release its flavour. However, it should not be overheated otherwise it will taste burnt.

Peppers (capsicums): These come in progressive stages of ripening, from green through yellow to red, but red ones, being the ripest, are sweeter and more rounded in flavour.

To remove the skin from peppers, (capsicums), either grill halved peppers (capsicums) skinside uppermost, 5 cm (2 in) away from the grill for 8-10 minutes, or bake them in an oven preheated to 200C (400F/Gas 6) for 20-40 minutes until they are blistered and charred (this also adds a delicious smoky flavour), leave until cool enough to handle, then scrape or peel off the skin.

Thin-skinned, small, long and pointed piquillo peppers (capsicums) are the ones that are used for stuffing; they are sold in bottles, which are generally best, or in cans. If unavailable, substitute ordinary canned small red peppers (capsicums).

Dark red *ñora* peppers (capsicums) are sold dried and can be seen in Spain in strings hanging from windows or in markets or grocers. They do not have much flesh, but their flavour and colour is concentrated. To use them, pull out the stalk and shake out as many seeds as possible. Soak them in cold water for 30-60 minutes to soften the skin, then cut in half and scrape out the flesh using a teaspoon. Paprika pepper can be substituted for *ñoras*.

Rice: Spanish rice is medium-grained, similar to Italian arborio (risotto) rice, but whereas a risotto is stirred to encourage the rice grains to become sticky, the rice for a paella must be left

undisturbed during cooking once the liquid has been added.

Saffron: Although expensive only a few threads are needed to give a wonderful flavour and aroma to a dish for four people. For the best flavour, use genuine Spanish saffron threads or strands, and avoid saffron powder as it may have added ingredients that give colour but no flavour. To gain maximum flavour from saffron, crush the threads with a small pestle and mortar or between two teaspoons, then soak in a little hot water.

Sherry vinegar: This is made from Spanish sherry, and is rich and concentrated, so very little is needed to enhance the flavour of a dish.

Tomatoes: Well-flavoured tomatoes are important to the success of many Spanish dishes. For the recipes in this book use irregular-shaped 'marmande' or beefsteak tomatoes, but avoid Dutch ones as they lack the flavour of those grown further south, under a hotter sun. To skin tomatoes, put them in a bowl, pour over boiling water, leave for about 30 seconds, then remove from the water one at a time and slip off the skin. It should come away easily.

EQUIPMENT

Pestle and mortar: This is used extensively, but the end of a rolling pin and a small bowl can be substituted for crushing spices and small amounts of ingredients, and a small blender or food processor for larger volumes.

Cazuelas: Cazuelas are earthenware casseroles that are unglazed outside and glazed inside. They are the most commonly used pieces of cooking equipment in Spain. *Cazuelas* are available in a wide variety of shapes, sizes and depths from fairly shallow small ones for individual portions of tapas, to deep ones used for poultry and meat casseroles. It is wise to use a heat diffuser when cooking on top of the stove as direct contact with heat can cause a *cazuela* to crack.

A *cazuela* should be seasoned before using it for the first time to avoid cracking: half fill with water and a generous splash of vinegar, bring gently to the boil, then boil until the liquid has evaporated. *Cazuela* rarely have lids but foil can be used for a covering.

Paella: Although a wide frying pan can be used for making paellas, a proper paella pan with a thick metal base and sloping sides is better.

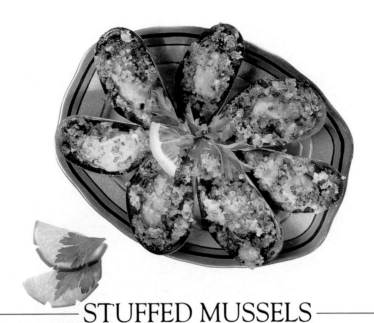

STUFFED MUSSELS

1.5 kg (3 lb) large mussels in their shells
85 ml (3 fl oz/⅓ cup) dry white wine
85 ml (3 fl oz/⅓ cup) olive oil
25 g (1 oz/½ cup) fresh breadcrumbs
3 tablespoons finely chopped fresh parsley
1 tablespoon finely chopped fresh oregano
2 cloves garlic, finely crushed
pinch cayenne pepper
salt and freshly ground black pepper
1 large lemon, quartered
parsley sprigs and lemon slices, to garnish

Scrub mussels and remove beards. Discard any mussels that remain open when tapped firmly. Put in a large saucepan with wine.

Cover and boil for 4-5 minutes, shaking pan occasionally, until shells open. Strain and reserve liquid. Discard any shells that do not open. Discard top shells, leaving mussels on remaining shells. In a small bowl, stir together 3 tablespoons oil, the breadcrumbs, herbs, garlic, cayenne and salt and pepper. Moisten with a little of the reserved mussel cooking liquid, if mixture is dry.

Preheat grill. Divide breadcrumb mixture between mussels on their shells. Place on a baking tray. Sprinkle with remaining olive oil and place under hot grill for 1-2 minutes until topping is crisp and golden. Squeeze over plenty of lemon juice and serve garnished with parsley sprigs and lemon slices.

Serves 4-6.

SIZZLING PRAWNS

100 ml (3½ fl oz/scant ½ cup) olive oil
4 cloves garlic, finely crushed
1 small fresh red chilli, seeded and chopped
350 g (12 oz) raw prawns, peeled
sea salt
2 tablespoons chopped fresh parsley
lemon wedges and bread, to serve

Heat oil in 4 individual flameproof earthen-ware dishes over a high heat. Add garlic and chilli, cook for 1-2 minutes, then add prawns and sea salt.

Cook briskly for 2-3 minutes. Stir in parsley. Serve quickly so the prawns are sizzling in the oil, and accompany with lemon wedges and bread to mop up the juices.

Note: One large dish, or a frying pan, can be used instead of individual dishes.

Serves 4.

GRILLED PRAWNS

450 g (1 lb) raw Mediterranean (king) prawns, peeled,
    leaving tail shells on
5 tablespoons extra virgin olive oil
½ clove garlic, finely crushed
juice 1 lemon
salt and freshly ground black pepper
1 small beefsteak tomato, peeled, seeded and finely
    chopped
½ small, fresh red chilli, finely chopped
1 tablespoon finely chopped fresh parsley
parsley sprigs and lemon slices and rind, to garnish

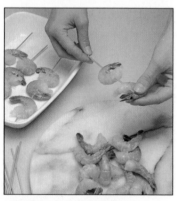

Using a small sharp knife, make a fine cut
along spine of each prawn and remove black
vein. Thread prawns onto small skewers and
place in a shallow dish. In a small bowl, stir
together 2 tablespoons oil, the garlic, 1½
tablespoons lemon juice and salt and pepper.
Pour over prawns and leave for 30 minutes.

Preheat grill. Lift prawns from dish and place
on grill rack; brush with any liquid remaining
in dish and grill for 3-4 minutes until bright
pink. In another small bowl, stir together
remaining oil and lemon juice, the tomato,
chilli, parsley and salt and pepper. Spoon
over hot prawns and serve garnished with
parsley sprigs and lemon slices and rind.

Serves 4.

——— PRAWNS IN OVERCOATS ———

450 g (1 lb) raw Mediterranean (king) prawns, peeled,
  leaving tail shells on
½ lemon
salt and freshly ground black pepper
200 g (7 oz/1¾ cups) plain flour
450 ml (16 fl oz/2 cups) light ale
olive oil for deep frying
lemon and lime wedges and dill, to garnish

Using a small sharp knife, make a fine cut
along spine of each prawn and remove black
vein. Squeeze lemon juice over prawns and
season lightly. Set aside for 15 minutes.

In a bowl, stir together flour and a small
pinch of salt. Slowly whisk in ale to make a
smooth, thick batter.

Two-thirds fill a deep fat fryer with oil and
heat to 180C (350F). Pat prawns dry with
absorbent kitchen paper. Pick up each prawn
in turn by its tail and dip in batter; do not
cover tail. Lower into oil and cook for about
4 minutes until crisp and golden. Drain on
absorbent kitchen paper and serve hot,
garnished with lemon and lime wedges and
dill.

Serves 4.

TUNA CROQUETTES

440 g (15½ oz) can tuna in brine
about 200 ml (7 fl oz/scant 1 cup) milk
2 tablespoons olive oil, plus extra for deep frying
¼ Spanish onion, finely chopped
4 tablespoons plain flour
1½ tablespoons finely chopped fresh parsley
2 tablespoons lemon juice
3 eggs, beaten
salt and freshly ground black pepper
175 g (6 oz/3 cups) fresh breadcrumbs
lemon wedges and watercress, to serve

Drain tuna and make up juice to 350 ml (12 fl oz/1½ cups) with milk. Flake tuna; set aside.

Heat 1 tablespoon olive oil in a small saucepan, add onion and cook for about 4 minutes until soft but not coloured. Stir in flour and cook, stirring, for 2 minutes. Remove from heat and slowly stir in half the milk mixture. Return to heat and bring to boil, stirring in remaining milk mixture. Simmer for 8 minutes, stirring occasionally. Off the heat, stir in tuna, parsley, lemon juice, 1 egg and salt and pepper.

Pour into a shallow dish, cool, cover and refrigerate for 2-3 hours. Put remaining eggs and the breadcrumbs into separate bowls. Dip small balls of tuna mixture first in egg then breadcrumbs to coat evenly. Half fill a deep fat fryer with oil and heat to 180C (350F). Fry tuna balls in batches for 2-3 minutes until crisp and golden. Using a slotted spoon, transfer to absorbent kitchen paper to drain. Serve hot with lemon wedges and small sprigs of watercress.

Serves 4.

STUFFED SQUID

750 g-1 kg (1½-2 lb) small squid
4 anchovy fillets, canned in oil, drained
55 g (2 oz) almonds, toasted and chopped, or 6 black
    olives, stoned and chopped
1 clove garlic, crushed
1½ tablespoons mixed chopped fresh parsley and
    oregano
1 egg, beaten
1 tablespoon ground almonds
salt and paprika
3 tablespoons olive oil
juice ½ lemon
lemon slices, stoned, sliced black olives and herb sprigs,
    to garnish

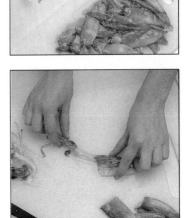

Preheat oven to 180C (350F/Gas 4). To prepare squid, cut off fins. Pull bag and tentacles
apart. Remove backbone and any soft innards
from bag. Cut head away from tentacles and
discard. Rinse bag and tentacles thoroughly
under cold running water. Chop tentacles
finely and place in a small bowl. Using a fork,
mix in anchovies, then chopped almonds
or olives, garlic, herbs, egg and ground
almonds. Season with salt and paprika.

Fill squid with anchovy mixture, secure
openings with wooden cocktail sticks, then
place in a single layer in a shallow baking
dish. Sprinkle with salt and paprika, then
pour the oil and lemon juice over the top.
Bake for about 30 minutes until tender. Serve
garnished with lemon slices, black olives and
herbs.

Serves 4-6.

GREEN MUSSEL SALAD

1.5 kg (3 lb) mussels in their shells
8 tablespoons virgin olive oil
2 tablespoons white wine vinegar
2 teaspoons capers
2 tablespoons finely chopped Spanish onion
½ clove garlic, finely chopped
2 tablespoons chopped fresh parsley
1 teaspoon paprika
small pinch cayenne pepper
salt

Clean mussels (see page 12). Put in a large saucepan with 5 tablespoons water, cover pan and boil for 4-5 minutes, shaking pan occasionally, until shells open. Drain mussels and discard any that remain closed. Remove mussels from shells and discard shells.

In a bowl, mix together remaining ingredients and mussels, cover and place in refrigerator overnight. Return to room temperature before serving.

Serves 4.

TUNA SALAD

200 g (7 oz) can tuna in brine, well drained and flaked
1 large green pepper (capsicum), peeled, seeded and
   diced
1 large red pepper (capsicum), peeled, seeded and diced
3 beefsteak tomatoes, peeled, seeded and diced
2 large hard-boiled eggs
1 thin slice day-old bread, crusts removed
1 clove garlic, finely chopped
salt and freshly ground black pepper
1 ½ tablespoons red wine vinegar
3 tablespoons olive oil
crisp lettuce leaves, to serve
parsley, to garnish

Put tuna, peppers (capsicums) and tomatoes
into a bowl. Peel eggs, chop whites (reserve
yolks) and add to bowl. Stir ingredients
together, cover and chill lightly.

Soak bread in cold water, then squeeze out.
Using a small blender or pestle and mortar,
mix garlic to a paste with salt and hard-boiled
egg yolks. Mix in bread, vinegar and pepper.
Slowly work in oil to make a smooth cream.
Pour over salad 30 minutes before serving. To
serve, toss salad gently and arrange on crisp
lettuce leaves. Garnish with parsley.

Serves 6.

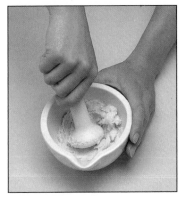

MARINATED SARDINES

450 g (1 lb) fresh sardines or anchovies, cleaned
sea salt and freshly ground black pepper
115 ml (4 fl oz/½ cup) white wine vinegar
1 clove garlic, finely crushed
2 tablespoons finely chopped Spanish onion
3 tablespoons olive oil
2 teaspoons lemon juice
diced peeled red pepper (capsicum) and chopped
   fresh parsley, to garnish

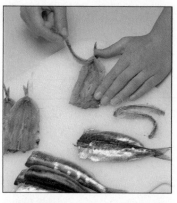

Place one fish skin-side uppermost on work surface and press thumbs firmly along backbone; turn fish over, pull out backbone from head and cut free at tail. Repeat with remaining fish.

Lay fish in a shallow, non-metallic dish. Sprinkle over sea salt, vinegar, garlic and onion. Cover and leave in a cool place overnight. Drain and rinse fish; reserve some of onion. Dry fish on absorbent kitchen paper, then place on a serving plate. In a small bowl, mix together oil, lemon juice, reserved onion and salt and pepper. Pour over fish and garnish with diced red pepper (capsicum) and parsley.

Serves 4.

CHEESE FRITTERS

olive oil for deep frying
2 egg whites
115 g (4 oz/1 cup) finely grated mature Manchego or
    Parmesan cheese
55 g (2 oz/1 cup) fresh breadcrumbs
about 1 tablespoon finely chopped fresh herbs, such as
    parsley, chives and thyme
salt, freshly ground black pepper and paprika
thyme sprigs, to garnish

Heat a deep fat fryer two thirds filled with
olive oil to 180C (350F).

Meanwhile, in a bowl, whisk egg whites until
stiff but not dry. Lightly fold in cheese, breadcrumbs and herbs. Season with salt, pepper
and paprika.

Form egg white mixture into small walnut-
size balls, adding balls to hot oil as they are
shaped. Fry for about 3 minutes until golden.
Transfer to absorbent kitchen paper to drain.
Serve hot, garnished with sprigs of thyme.

Serves 4.

—RED PEPPER & ONION TART—

225 g (8 oz / 2 cups) strong flour
salt and freshly ground black pepper
1 teaspoon easy-blend yeast
150 ml (5 fl oz / ⅔ cup) milk
1 egg yolk
4 tablespoons olive oil
450 g (1 lb) Spanish onions, halved and sliced
4 red peppers (capsicums), seeded and sliced
4 yellow peppers (capsicums), seeded and sliced
handful thyme, oregano and parsley sprigs
16-20 canned anchovy fillets, drained

Sift flour and salt into a bowl. Stir in yeast.

Stir milk into egg yolk then slowly pour into flour, stirring constantly. Beat for 5-10 minutes, until dough comes cleanly away from bowl.

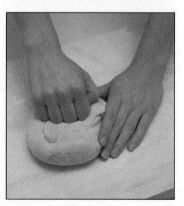

Turn dough onto a lightly floured surface and knead until smooth and elastic. Form into a ball, place in an oiled bowl, cover and leave in a warm place for about 1 hour, until doubled in volume.

Meanwhile, heat 3 tablespoons oil in a large non-stick frying pan, add onions, peppers (capsicums) and herbs and cook over a moderate heat, stirring occasionally, for 20-25 minutes, until vegetables are soft but not browned. Add a few tablespoons water if necessary to prevent browning. Season and set aside.

Preheat oven to 240C (475F/Gas 9). On a lightly floured surface, punch down and flatten dough. Roll out to a 30 cm (12 in) circle. Curl up edge to make a lip. Carefully transfer to an oiled baking tray. Prick well.

Spread vegetable mixture over dough, arrange anchovy fillets on top, trickle over remaining oil and bake for 25-30 minutes, until the dough is well risen, crisp and golden. Serve warm.

Serves 6.

EMPANADA

450 g (1 lb/4 cups) strong flour
salt
2 teaspoons easy-blend dried yeast
300 ml (10 fl oz/1¼ cups) tepid milk
2 egg yolks
dash anise
1 egg, beaten
FILLING:
2 tablespoons olive oil
2 Spanish onions, chopped
225 g (8 oz) beefsteak tomatoes
400 g (14 oz) can tuna in oil, drained
1 large red pepper (capsicum)
6 black olives, stoned and quartered
4 saffron threads

Sift flour and pinch of salt into a bowl. Stir in yeast. Stir milk into egg yolks, add anise, then slowly pour into flour, stirring constantly. Beat for 5-10 minutes until dough comes cleanly away from bowl.

Turn onto a lightly floured surface and knead until smooth and elastic. Form into 2 even-sized balls, place in an oiled bowl, cover and leave in a warm place until doubled in volume, about 1 hour.

To make filling, heat oil in a frying pan, add onions and cook, stirring occasionally, for about 4 minutes until softened. Peel, seed and chop tomatoes, stir into pan and simmer until thickened. Flake tuna. Peel and chop pepper (capsicum) and stir into pan with tuna and olives. Crush saffron threads and dissolve in 2 tablespoons hot water. Add to pan. Simmer until well combined, then set aside.

Preheat oven to 200C (400F/Gas 6). Grease a baking sheet. On a lightly floured surface, roll out each piece of dough to a thin rectangle or square. Transfer one piece to baking sheet.

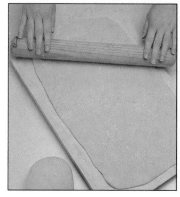

Spread filling over dough, leaving a narrow border clear all the way round. Dampen border with water. Cover with the other piece of dough and press edges together. Glaze with beaten egg and cut a slit in centre. Bake for 15-20 minutes until golden. Serve warm, cut into rectangles or squares.

Serves 4-6.

KIDNEYS IN SHERRY

450 g (1 lb) lambs' kidneys
3 tablespoons olive oil
2 cloves garlic, chopped
115 g (4 oz) mushrooms, chopped
55 g (2 oz) serrano ham, sliced
salt and freshly ground black pepper
6-8 tablespoons fino sherry
parsley, to garnish

Remove skin from outside of kidneys. Cut each kidney in half lengthways, then snip out and discard cores. Quarter the kidneys, then set them aside.

Heat oil in a frying pan, add garlic and cook for 2-3 minutes. Stir in mushrooms and ham and fry until liquid from mushrooms has evaporated.

Stir kidneys into pan and fry for 2-3 minutes, stirring frequently, so kidneys are lightly browned on outside and still pink in centre. Add seasoning and sherry and boil, stirring occasionally, until sherry has almost evaporated. Garnish with parsley and serve hot.

Serves 4.

────── SPICY PORK KEBABS ──────

2 teaspoons paprika
1 teaspoon finely crushed coriander seeds
1½ teaspoons ground cumin
1 teaspoon finely chopped fresh oregano
¼ teaspoon ground ginger
large pinch each ground cinnamon, cayenne pepper and
   grated nutmeg
1 bay leaf, finely crumbled
2 tablespoons olive oil
salt and freshly ground black pepper
450 g (1 lb) boned loin of pork, cut into 2.5 cm
   (1 in) cubes
lemon slices and bay leaves, to garnish

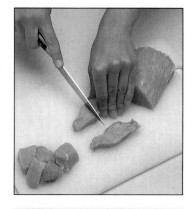

In a bowl, mix together all ingredients, except pork and garnish. Add pork and stir to coat evenly with marinade. Cover bowl and leave in refrigerator for 8-12 hours, turning pork occasionally.

Preheat grill. Thread the pork onto small skewers. Cook under hot grill for about 7 minutes, turning occasionally, until pork is cooked through but still juicy. Garnish with lemon slices and bay leaves and serve hot.

Serves 4.

SPICY OLIVES

450 g (1 lb) green or black olives
1 sprig oregano
1 sprig thyme
1 teaspoon finely chopped fresh rosemary
2 bay leaves
1 teaspoon fennel seeds, bruised
1 teaspoon finely crushed cumin seeds
1 fresh red chilli, seeded and chopped
4 cloves garlic, crushed
olive oil to cover

Using a small sharp knife, make a lengthways slit through to stone of each olive. Put olives into a bowl. Stir in oregano, thyme, rosemary, bay leaves, fennel seeds, cumin, chilli and garlic.

Pack olive mixture into a screw-top or preserving jar. Pour over sufficient oil to cover, close the lid and leave for at least 3 days, shaking jar occasionally, before using.

Serves 6.

— MUSHROOMS WITH GARLIC —

3 tablespoons olive oil
2 cloves garlic, finely chopped
450 g (1 lb) mushrooms, cut into large pieces
4 tablespoons fino sherry
55 g (2 oz) pine nuts
squeeze lemon juice
salt and freshly ground black pepper
2 tablespoons chopped fresh parsley

In a large frying pan, heat oil, add garlic and cook over a fairly high heat for about 3 minutes until just beginning to brown.

Stir mushrooms, sherry and pine nuts into pan and continue to cook until mushroom juices have almost evaporated. Add lemon juice and seasonings to taste, then stir in parsley and serve.

Serves 4.

ANCHOVY-STUFFED MUSHROOMS

25 g (1 oz) fresh bread without crusts, crumbled
4 tablespoons milk
450 g (1 lb) medium cap mushrooms
115 g (4 oz) green (unsmoked) bacon, finely chopped
4 canned anchovy fillets, finely chopped
1 clove garlic, finely chopped
1 egg, beaten
3 tablespoons finely chopped fresh parsley
pinch chopped fresh oregano
salt and freshly ground black pepper
4 tablespoons dry breadcrumbs
4 tablespoons olive oil
oregano sprigs, to garnish

Preheat oven to 200C (400F/Gas 6). Oil a
large baking tray. Put fresh bread in a small
bowl, add milk and leave to soak. Remove
stalks from mushrooms and chop finely. Put
into a bowl with bacon, anchovy fillets,
garlic, egg, parsley, oregano and salt and
pepper. Squeeze soaked bread dry, add to
bacon mixture and mix together well.

Divide bread mixture between open side of
mushroom caps, piling mixture into small
mounds. Place on baking tray and sprinkle
with dry breadcrumbs. Trickle oil over mushrooms. Bake on top shelf of oven for 20-30
minutes until top of stuffing is crisp. Leave
to stand for a few minutes before serving,
garnished with oregano.

Serves 4-6.

PRAWN-STUFFED EGGS

4 hard-boiled eggs, peeled
4 tablespoons mayonnaise
55 g (2 oz) peeled prawns, chopped
salt, cayenne pepper and lemon juice, to taste
lettuce leaves, to serve
whole prawns, paprika and parsley sprigs, to garnish

Slice the eggs in half lengthways. Using a teaspoon, scoop the yolks into a small bowl; reserve the white shells.

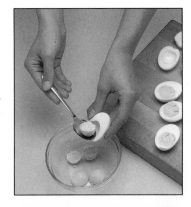

Add the mayonnaise to the bowl and, using a fork, mash with the yolks and prawns. Add salt, cayenne pepper and lemon juice to taste.

Divide the prawn mixture between the egg whites. Arrange on lettuce leaves and garnish with whole prawns, paprika and parsley sprigs.

Serves 4.

——CAULIFLOWER FRITTERS——

1 small head cauliflower, about 750 g (1½ lb)
40 g (1½ oz/⅓ cup) plain flour
40 g (1½ oz/⅓ cup) freshly grated Manchego or
    Parmesan cheese
salt and freshly ground black pepper
1 egg, beaten
115 ml (4 fl oz/½ cup) light ale
olive oil for deep frying
chopped herbs, to garnish

Cook cauliflower in boiling salted water for about 20 minutes until tender but still very firm. Drain and divide into florets. Cut each floret in half.

Put flour, cheese, pepper and a little salt into a small bowl. Stir together, then form a well in centre. Pour egg into well. Gradually pour in beer, drawing dry ingredients into liquids. Leave to stand for 30 minutes.

Half-fill a deep fat fryer or a pan with olive oil and heat to 180C (350F). Dip 2 or 3 pieces of cauliflower into batter, allow excess batter to flow off, then slip them into pan. Add more pieces to pan, but do not crowd. Cook for 2-3 minutes until cauliflower has a nice golden crust, then using a slotted spoon, transfer to absorbent kitchen paper to drain. Continue until all cauliflower has been cooked. Serve hot, garnished with chopped herbs.

Serves 6-8.

STUFFED PEPPERS

250 g (9 oz) minced chicken
2 slices lightly smoked bacon, chopped
75 g (3 oz) button brown cap mushrooms, finely
  chopped
1 clove garlic, finely chopped
1 tablespoon olive oil, plus extra for frying
2 tablespoons seasoned plain flour, plus extra for
  coating
3 tablespoons milk
2½ tablespoons finely chopped fresh parsley
pinch freshly grated nutmeg
12-16 bottled or canned small red peppers (capsicums)
  or piquillo, drained
2 large eggs, beaten
parsley sprigs, to garnish
1 quantity Tomato Sauce, see page 115, to serve

In a bowl, mix together chicken, bacon,
mushrooms and garlic. Heat 1 tablespoon oil
in a frying pan, add chicken mixture and
cook, stirring occasionally, for 2-3 minutes.
Stir in the 2 tablespoons flour, cook for
2 minutes, then stir in milk, parsley and
nutmeg. Cook for 2-3 minutes, stirring frequently. Cool, then divide between peppers
(capsicums).

Put eggs on a deep plate and seasoned flour on
another plate. Dip peppers (capsicums) in
egg, then flour to coat lightly and evenly.
Heat a 0.5-1 cm (¼-½ in) layer of oil in a
frying pan, add peppers (capsicums) and fry
until evenly browned, about 4 minutes, turning peppers (capsicums) carefully. Using a
slotted spoon, transfer to absorbent kitchen
paper to drain. Garnish with sprigs of parsley
and serve hot with Tomato Sauce.

Serves 4.

——POTATOES WITH ALLIOLI——

450 g (1 lb) small potatoes, preferably new, unpeeled
sea salt
1 tablespoon finely chopped fresh parsley
ALLIOLI SAUCE:
6-9 cloves garlic
salt and freshly ground black pepper
about 150 ml (5 fl oz/⅔ cup) olive oil

Add potatoes to a saucepan of boiling salted water and boil until tender.

Meanwhile, make sauce. Using a pestle and mortar, crush garlic with a little salt. Work in oil a drop at a time; as the sauce thickens the oil can be added more quickly. Season with salt and pepper.

Drain potatoes well. Immediately potatoes are cool enough to handle, cut into bite-size chunks and toss with sea salt and the allioli. Sprinkle with parsley and serve warm.

Serves 4-6.

Variation: Pound 1 egg yolk with the garlic, then add juice of ½ lemon to finished sauce.

—POTATOES WITH RED SAUCE—

1 kg (2 lb) walnut-size new potatoes, unpeeled
25 g (1 oz) sea salt
SAUCE:
4 large cloves garlic
salt
1 teaspoon cumin seeds
1 teaspoon paprika
1/2 teaspoon chopped fresh thyme
150 ml (5 fl oz/2/3 cup) olive oil
2 teaspoons white wine vinegar
3 tablespoons warm water

To make sauce, using a pestle and mortar, crush garlic and a pinch of salt to a pulp.

Add cumin, paprika and thyme and crush well. Gradually mix in oil and vinegar, as for making mayonnaise. Stir in warm water and set aside to cool completely.

Boil potatoes in an uncovered saucepan, in just enough water to cover them. When most of water has evaporated, add the sea salt, which will form a crust on the skins. Allow water to boil away over a low heat until it has all evaporated. Leave on heat for about 30 seconds to dry potatoes thoroughly and produce a wrinkled effect; shake pan a little if potatoes start to burn. Serve in individual dishes accompanied by sauce.

Serves 4.

—SPANISH VEGETABLE SALAD—

2 Spanish onions, unpeeled
450 g (1 lb) small aubergines (eggplants)
2 red peppers (capsicums)
3 firm but ripe beefsteak tomatoes
8 cloves garlic
10 g (⅓ oz) cumin seeds
juice 1 lemon
4 tablespoons virgin olive oil
3 tablespoons white wine vinegar
salt
2 tablespoons finely chopped fresh parsley (optional)

Preheat oven to 180C (350F/Gas 4). Place onions on a baking sheet and bake for 10 minutes. Add aubergines (eggplants).

Bake for another 10 minutes, then add peppers (capsicums). Bake for 10 minutes before adding tomatoes and 6 of the garlic cloves and cooking for a further 15 minutes, until all vegetables tender. If necessary, remove any cooked vegetables from oven. When vegetables are cool enough to handle, peel them with your fingers.

Cut core and seeds from peppers (capsicums) then cut flesh into strips. Halve tomatoes, discard seeds then slice flesh. Slice aubergines (eggplants) into strips, onions into rings. Arrange in a serving dish. Using a pestle and mortar, pound to a paste the roasted and the raw garlic and the cumin seeds. Beat in lemon juice, oil and vinegar. Add salt to taste. Pour over vegetables and sprinkle with parsley, if desired. Serve warm or cold.

Serves 4.

ROAST PEPPER SALAD

4 red peppers (capsicums), peeled, seeded and cut into
   strips
4 canned anchovy fillets, cut lengthways into slivers
1 tablespoon capers (optional)
1 tablespoon finely chopped fresh parsley
8 tablespoons virgin olive oil
salt and freshly ground black pepper

Place peppers (capsicums) in a shallow dish.
Arrange anchovy fillets on top and sprinkle
with capers, if using.

In a small bowl, beat together parsley, oil,
pepper and just a little salt, if liked. Trickle
the dressing over peppers (capsicums),
anchovies and capers.

Serves 4.

LEEK SALAD

8 long, slim leeks
1 small red pepper (capsicum), peeled, seeded and cut
  into strips
4 tablespoons white wine vinegar
115 ml (4 fl oz/½ cup) virgin olive oil
pinch caster sugar
large pinch paprika
salt and freshly ground black pepper
chopped fresh parsley, capers (optional) and stoned oil-
  cured black olives, to garnish

Cook leeks in boiling salted water for about 6
minutes until just tender but still firm.

Meanwhile, in a bowl, mix together red
pepper (capsicum), vinegar, oil, sugar,
paprika and salt and pepper. Drain leeks well,
briefly lay on absorbent kitchen paper to
absorb excess moisture, then place in a warm,
shallow dish.

Pour over vinegar mixture, turn leeks to coat
well, then cover and leave for a few hours in a
cool place, turning leeks occasionally.
Garnish with chopped parsley, capers, if
using, and black olives.

Serves 4.

────── VEGETABLE SALAD ──────

450 g (1 lb) potatoes, unpeeled
1 large carrot, peeled and halved or quartered
55 g (2 oz) peas
115 g (4 oz) green beans
2 tablespoons chopped Spanish onion
1 small red pepper (capsicum), peeled, seeded and
  chopped
4 small pickled gherkins, chopped
1½ tablespoons capers
8-12 black or anchovy-stuffed olives
150 ml (5 fl oz/⅔ cup) mayonnaise
1 hard-boiled egg, sliced
chopped fresh parsley, to garnish

Boil potatoes in their skins until tender.
Cool, peel, then cut into dice. Boil carrot,
peas and beans. Dice carrot and cut beans
into short lengths.

Put potatoes, carrot, peas and beans into a
bowl and stir in onion, pepper (capsicum),
gherkins, capers, olives and mayonnaise
while vegetables are still warm. Leave to
cool. Arrange hard-boiled egg and chopped
parsley on top before serving.

Serves 4.

— WHITE SOUP WITH GRAPES —

200 g (7 oz) shelled almonds
4 slices day-old, firm white bread, crusts removed,
 soaked in cold water and squeezed dry
3 cloves garlic, crushed
115 ml (4 fl oz/½ cup) olive oil
2-3 tablespoons sherry vinegar
salt
225 g (8 oz) muscat or other well-flavoured grapes,
 peeled and seeded, if necessary
chopped fresh parsley, to garnish

Place almonds in a bowl and pour over boiling water. Leave for 30 seconds, then remove nuts and squeeze them so the nuts pop out of their skins. Place nuts, bread and garlic in a food processor or blender and mix until smooth. With motor running, slowly pour in the oil. Add sufficient cold water, about 550 ml (20 fl oz/2½ cups), to give a creamy consistency.

Add vinegar and salt to taste. Add grapes and chill well. Pour into a cold soup tureen or individual soup bowls. Serve garnished with chopped parsley.

Serves 4-6.

GAZPACHO

750 g (1½ lb) beefsteak tomatoes
½ Spanish onion, chopped
1 green pepper (capsicum), chopped
1 red pepper (capsicum), chopped
2 cloves garlic, chopped
2 slices firm white bread, crusts removed, broken into
   pieces
300 ml (10 fl oz/1¼ cups) tomato juice
3 tablespoons virgin olive oil
2 tablespoons sherry vinegar
salt and freshly ground black pepper
about 8 ice cubes, to serve
ACCOMPANIMENTS:
1 diced small red pepper (capsicum), 1 diced small
   green pepper (capsicum), 1 diced small onion,
   1 chopped hard-boiled egg and croûtons

Peel, seed and chop tomatoes. Put in a food processor or blender with remaining soup ingredients, except ice cubes. Mix until smooth. Pour soup through a nylon sieve, pressing down well on contents of sieve. If necessary, thin soup with cold water, then chill well.

Place accompaniments in separate bowls. Adjust seasoning of soup, if necessary, then pour into cold soup bowls. Add ice cubes and serve with accompaniments.

Serves 4.

Variation: Do not sieve the soup if more texture is preferred.

—LENTIL & CHORIZO POTAJE—

450 g (1 lb) green or brown lentils
1 Spanish onion, chopped
2 carrots, chopped
6 cloves garlic
175-225 g (6-8 oz) cooking chorizo
115 g (4 oz) piece belly pork, rind removed
1 bay leaf
2 beefsteak tomatoes, peeled, seeded and chopped
1 red pepper (capsicum), seeded and chopped
1½ tablespoons olive oil
1 Spanish onion, finely chopped
salt and freshly ground black pepper

Put lentils, chopped onion, carrots, garlic, chorizo, pork, bay leaf, tomatoes and pepper (capsicum) into a flameproof casserole or a saucepan. Just cover with water and bring to boil. Cover and simmer gently for about 30 minutes until lentils are tender, pork is cooked and there is sufficient liquid left to make a thick soup.

Meanwhile, heat oil in a heavy-based casserole, add finely chopped onion and cook very gently for about 15 minutes, stirring occasionally, until soft and lightly caramelised. Stir into lentils and season with salt and pepper. Discard bay leaf. Slice chorizo and pork and return to lentils and heat through.

Serves 4-5.

SPICY CHICK PEA POTAJE

225 g (8 oz) chick peas, soaked overnight, then drained
4 tablespoons olive oil
1 slice bread, crusts removed
1 Spanish onion, finely chopped
225 g (8 oz) cooking chorizo, thickly sliced
3 beefsteak tomatoes, peeled, seeded and chopped
1 tablespoon paprika
¼-½ teaspoon cumin seeds, finely crushed
450 g (1 lb) spinach, trimmed and chopped
3 cloves garlic

Cook chick peas in 1½ times their volume of boiling water for 1½-2 hours until tender.

Meanwhile, heat 2 tablespoons oil in a small frying pan, add bread and fry until golden on both sides. Remove and drain on absorbent kitchen paper. Add onion to pan and cook slowly, stirring occasionally, for 5 minutes. Add chorizo and cook for further 5-10 minutes until onion has softened but not coloured. Stir tomatoes into onion and cook, stirring occasionally, for about 10 minutes.

Heat remaining oil in a saucepan, stir in paprika and cumin, then add spinach. Cook until spinach has wilted. Using a pestle and mortar, pound garlic with a pinch of salt. Add fried bread and pound again. Drain chick peas, reserving liquid. Stir chick peas into spinach with tomato and garlic mixtures, and 175 ml (6 fl oz/¾ cup) chick pea liquid. Cover pan and simmer for about 30 minutes; add more liquid if mixture becomes too dry.

Serves 4.

—SCRAMBLED EGGS & PRAWNS—

2 tablespoons olive oil
225 g (8 oz) mixed brown cap, shiitake and oyster
   mushrooms, sliced
1-2 tablespoons brandy
salt and freshly ground black pepper
400 g (14 oz) raw prawns, peeled
4 eggs, lightly beaten
2 tablespoons chopped fresh parsley

In a wide frying pan, heat oil and add mushrooms.

Sprinkle over brandy and salt and pepper and cook over a fairly high heat until the liquid has evaporated. Stir in prawns and cook, stirring, for 2 minutes.

Reduce heat to low, pour in eggs, add parsley and cook, stirring gently, until eggs are nearly set, but still creamy. Serve immediately on warm plates.

Serves 2-3.

HUEVOS FLAMENCA

2 tablespoons olive oil
½ Spanish onion, finely chopped
2 cloves garlic, crushed
4 slices serrano ham, chopped
1 small red pepper (capsicum), seeded and finely
    chopped
pinch paprika
1 large beefsteak tomato, peeled, seeded and chopped
85 g (3 oz/¾ cup) cooked fresh peas, or frozen peas
115 g (4 oz) cooked green beans
1 teaspoon tomato purée (paste), (optional)
salt and freshly ground black pepper
4 eggs
4 slices cooking chorizo
1 tablespoon chopped fresh parsley

Preheat oven to 230C (450F/Gas 8). In a
frying pan, heat oil, add onion and garlic and
cook for about 4 minutes, stirring occasionally, until softened but not browned. Add
half the ham and the pepper (capsicum). Fry
for 2 minutes, then stir in paprika. Heat for
1 minute. Add tomato. Simmer for about 10
minutes until reduced to a fairly thick purée.
Add peas and beans, and a little tomato purée
(paste) if necessary. Season.

Pour into a shallow ovenproof dish, or
4 individual dishes. Form 4 shallow depressions in mixture. Carefully break eggs into
depressions, allowing whites to flow over
surface. Scatter remaining ham over the top
and lay a chorizo slice on yolks. Bake for 8-10
minutes until egg whites are just set and yolks
still moist, or for about 15 minutes if firmer
eggs are preferred. Sprinkle with parsley and
serve.

Serves 4.

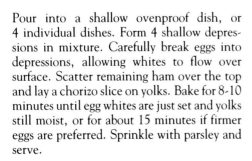

– ARTICHOKE & HAM TORTILLA –

3 artichokes
4 tablespoons olive oil
115 g (4 oz) serrano ham, finely diced
salt and freshly ground black pepper
6 eggs, lightly beaten

Trim artichokes to make artichoke bottoms, see page 50. Using a small sharp knife, cut each bottom into 8 pieces.

In a large frying pan, heat oil, add the artichoke pieces, ham and a little salt. Fry fairly gently for about 15 minutes, stirring occasionally, until artichoke pieces are just soft. Add black pepper. Stir in eggs, spreading mixture evenly in pan. Cook over moderate heat, shaking pan occasionally, until underside is set and beginning to brown.

Cover pan with a large plate and hold in place with one hand. Quickly turn pan upside down so omelette falls onto plate. Return pan to heat, add a little more oil, then slide omelette into pan, cooked side uppermost. Cook until lightly browned underneath. Slide onto a serving plate. Serve warm or at room temperature.

Serves 4 as a main course, or 8 as a tapa.

Note: Brown the omelette under the grill instead of turning over, if preferred.

— TORTILLA WITH RED PEPPER —

6 tablespoons olive oil
450 g (1 lb) potatoes, diced
1 Spanish onion, chopped
1 red pepper (capsicum), seeded and chopped
5 eggs
1 tablespoon chopped fresh parsley
salt and freshly ground black pepper

Heat oil in a large, heavy frying pan, prefer-ably non-stick. Add potatoes, onion and red pepper (capsicum) to pan. Cover and cook over a low heat for 15-20 minutes until soft but not brown, stirring occasionally to prevent sticking.

Drain off and reserve oil. In a bowl, lightly beat eggs. Mix in potatoes, onion and red pepper (capsicum) and chopped parsley. Season. Leave for 10 minutes. Wipe pan with absorbent kitchen paper. Add sufficient reserved oil to cover base in a thin film. Add egg mixture, spreading it evenly in pan. Cook over moderate heat, shaking pan occasion-ally, until underside is set and beginning to brown.

Cover pan with a large plate and hold in place with one hand. Quickly turn pan upside down so omelette falls onto plate. Return pan to heat, add a little more oil, then slide omelette into pan, cooked side uppermost (see Note opposite). Cook until lightly browned underneath. Slide onto a serving plate. Serve warm or at room temperature.

Serves 4 as a main course, or 8 as a tapa.

—MONKFISH WITH PAPRIKA—

750 g (1 ½ lb) skinned and filleted monkfish, cut into
    4 cm (1 ½ in) pieces
6 cloves garlic, crushed
1 tablespoon paprika
4 tablespoons olive oil
salt and freshly ground black pepper
115 ml (4 fl oz/½ cup) full-bodied dry white wine
chives and lemon wedges, to garnish

Put monkfish into a bowl. In a small bowl,
mix together garlic, paprika, 2 tablespoons
oil, salt and pepper.

Pour the mixture over the fish, stir to coat the
fish, then set aside for 30 minutes.

In a frying pan, heat remaining oil. Lift fish
from bowl, add to pan and cook for 2-3
minutes, stirring once or twice. Add any
mixture remaining in bowl and the wine.
Cook for about 5-7 minutes until fish flakes
when pierced with a knife. Serve garnished
with chives and lemon wedges.

Serves 4.

– MONKFISH & ALMOND SAUCE –

5 tablespoons olive oil
½ Spanish onion, finely chopped
1 kg (2 lb) monkfish tail, skinned and cut into
　　8 slices
salt and freshly ground black pepper
2 cloves garlic, crushed
12 blanched almonds, toasted and finely ground
1 tablespoon chopped fresh parsley
pinch saffron threads, finely crushed
2 tablespoons dry white wine, fish stock or water
225 g (8 oz) shelled fresh peas, or frozen peas
strips lemon rind and herbs, to garnish

Heat 2 tablespoons oil in a flameproof casserole, add onion and cook for 2-3 minutes.
Season monkfish and place on onion, spoon
over remaining oil and cook for 5 minutes.

Meanwhile, using a pestle and mortar, pound
garlic, almonds, parsley and saffron together
to make a smooth paste. Stir in wine, stock or
water. Spoon over monkfish, add fresh peas
to casserole and cook for 7-10 minutes until
fish flakes when pierced with a knife and peas
are tender. If using frozen peas, add about 3
minutes before end of cooking time. Serve
garnished with strips of lemon rind and herbs.

Serves 4.

— MONKFISH & ARTICHOKES —

4 tablespoons white wine vinegar
4 globe artichokes
2 tablespoons olive oil
550 g (1¼ lb) monkfish fillets, cut into 4 cm (1½ in) slices
salt and freshly ground black pepper
1 small Spanish onion, finely chopped
4 cloves garlic, chopped
225 ml (8 fl oz/1 cup) full-bodied dry white wine
1.25 kg (2½ lb) tomatoes
8 oil-cured black olives, stoned and halved
2 teaspoons capers
1 bay leaf
1 tablespoon chopped fresh parsley

Pour a depth of about 5 cm (2 in) water into a saucepan and add vinegar. Break or cut off stalk of one artichoke. Snap off and discard outer leaves, starting at base and continuing until pale yellow leaves are reached. Cut top two thirds off artichoke. Using a small, sharp knife, pare off any dark green leave bases that remain on the artichoke bottom. Cut the bottom into quarters; trim away any purple leaves and remove hairy choke. Cut each quarter into 4. Drop into pan.

Repeat with remaining artichokes, then simmer for about 15 minutes until tender. Drain and set aside.

Heat oil in a frying pan over a high heat, add fish and sear on each side for 1 minute. Transfer to a plate and season. Add onion to pan, lower heat to moderate and cook onion for about 4 minutes, stirring occasionally, until softened but not coloured. Stir in garlic, cook for 1 minute, then add wine and boil until almost evaporated.

Stir in tomatoes, olives, capers, bay leaf and parsley. Boil for about 10 minutes until reduced by a half.

Add artichokes and place monkfish on top. Reduce heat to moderate, cover pan and cook until fish flakes easily, about 10 minutes. Transfer fish to a warm plate. Boil sauce to thicken slightly, adjust seasoning and pour over fish.

Serves 4.

—ROAST MONKFISH & GARLIC—

1 kg (2 lb) monkfish tail or two 450 g (1 lb) pieces,
   skinned
2 heads plump garlic, divided into cloves
2 tablespoons olive oil
salt and freshly ground black pepper
1/4 teaspoon fresh thyme leaves
1/4 teaspoon fennel seeds
juice 1 lemon
1 bay leaf
1 large red pepper (capsicum), peeled, seeded and cut
   into strips

Preheat oven to 220C (425F/Gas 7). Make
sure membrane has been removed from fish.
Cut out bone, then tie fish back into shape.

Using the point of a sharp knife, make some
incisions in fish. Cut 2 garlic cloves into thin
slices and push into incisions. Heat 1 tablespoon oil in a frying pan, add fish and brown
on all sides for about 5 minutes. Remove and
season with salt, pepper, thyme, fennel and
lemon juice.

Place fish on bay leaf in roasting tin. Arrange
remaining garlic around fish. Bake for 15
minutes. Add pepper (capsicum) strips and
cook for about 5 minutes until fish flakes
when pierced with a knife. Arrange fish,
garlic, pepper (capsicum) and cooking juices
on a plate. Carve fish in thin slices.

Serves 4.

— SOLE WITH GREEN DRESSING —

flour for coating
salt and freshly ground black pepper
1 egg, lightly beaten
about 100 g (3½ oz/1½ cups) fresh breadcrumbs
4 fillets sole or plaice, about 175 g (6 oz) each
4 tablespoons olive oil
lemon wedges and fresh herbs, to garnish
GREEN DRESSING:
3 cloves garlic
6 canned anchovy fillets, chopped
3 tablespoons finely chopped fresh parsley
½ teaspoon chopped fresh oregano
1½ tablespoons finely chopped capers
1½ tablespoons lemon juice
150 ml (5 fl oz/⅔ cup) virgin olive oil

To make the dressing, using a pestle and
mortar, crush garlic with anchovies, then
mix in parsley, oregano, capers and lemon
juice. Beat in oil very slowly; set aside. Put
flour on a plate and season with salt and
pepper. Put egg and breadcrumbs on separate
plates. Coat fish in seasoned flour, then dip
in egg. Allow excess to drain off, then coat
fish lightly and evenly in breadcrumbs. Set
aside for 5 minutes.

Heat oil in a large frying pan, add fish and
cook until golden and crisp and flesh flakes
easily, about 3 minutes each side. Cook fish
in batches if necessary so pan is not crowded.
Using a fish slice, transfer fish to absorbent
kitchen paper to drain. Garnish with lemon
wedges and herbs. Stir dressing and serve
with hot fish.

Serves 4.

TROUT WITH HAM

4 trout, about 300 g (10 oz) each, cleaned
salt and freshly ground black pepper
4 tablespoons olive oil
115 g (4 oz) serrano ham, finely chopped
2 cloves garlic, finely chopped
1 tablespoon chopped fresh parsley
juice 1 lemon
parsley sprigs, to garnish

Season skin and inside cavities of each trout with salt and pepper.

Heat 2 tablespoons oil in a large frying pan, add trout, in batches if necessary, and fry for about 6 minutes until flesh flakes when pierced with the point of a sharp knife. Transfer to a warm plate, cover and keep warm.

Put remaining oil in small saucepan, add ham and garlic and cook, stirring occasionally, until beginning to brown. Stir in parsley and lemon juice and heat for a few minutes. Pour the mixture over the trout. Serve garnished with parsley sprigs.

Serves 4.

MULLET WITH ANCHOVY SAUCE

4 red mullet, about 225 g (8 oz) each, scaled and
  cleaned
8 canned anchovy fillets, rinsed
flour for coating
salt and freshly ground black pepper
115 ml (4 fl oz/½ cup) freshly squeezed orange juice
4 tablespoons skinned, seeded and chopped tomato
chopped fresh parsley, capers and 1 orange, peeled and
  divided into segments, to garnish

Preheat grill. Using the point of a sharp
knife, cut 2 diagonal slashes in both sides of
each fish. Cut 4 anchovy fillets into 4 pieces
and insert one piece in each slash. Roughly
chop remaining anchovy fillets. Season flour
with salt and pepper, then coat fish lightly
and evenly.

Brush fish with oil, then place under very hot
grill until crisp and flesh flakes easily, about 5
minutes each side. Transfer to a warm serving
plate and keep warm. Stir orange juice,
tomato and chopped anchovies into juices
in grill pan, then pour into a saucepan, place
over direct heat and bubble until thickened
to a light sauce. Add pepper. Pour sauce
around fish and garnish with parsley, capers
and orange segments.

Serves 4.

——HALIBUT IN WHITE SAUCE——

4 tablespoons olive oil
flour for coating
salt and freshly ground black pepper
1 kg (2 lb) halibut, cut into 2.5 cm (1 in) thick slices
½ Spanish onion, finely chopped
2 canned anchovy fillets, coarsely chopped
3 tablespoons chopped fresh parsley
175 ml (6 fl oz/¾ cup) dry white wine
squeeze lemon juice

Heat 3 tablespoons oil in a large frying pan. Put flour on a plate and season with salt and pepper. Coat fish evenly in the seasoned flour. Add fish slices to pan, making sure they are not crowded. Cook for 5 minutes each side.

Meanwhile, heat remaining oil in a small saucepan; add onion and cook gently for about 7 minutes until lightly coloured. Add anchovies and parsley and cook, stirring and mashing anchovies with a wooden spoon until dissolved. Stir in wine and boil until reduced by half. Add pepper and lemon juice to taste. Spoon or pour surplus oil from frying pan, then pour the anchovy sauce over the fish. Leave over moderate heat for 2 minutes, basting fish occasionally, then serve.

Serves 4.

– HAKE WITH PEAS & POTATOES –

½ Spanish onion, thinly sliced
8 cloves garlic, sliced
4 potatoes, thinly sliced
3 sprigs parsley
1 bay leaf
salt
4 hake steaks, about 225 g (8 oz) each
225 g (8 oz) shelled fresh peas, or frozen peas
6 tablespoons olive oil
1 tablespoon paprika

Put onion, 2 cloves garlic, the potatoes, parsley and bay leaf in a heavy flameproof casserole.

Just cover with cold water, add salt and simmer for 10 minutes. Add hake and fresh peas and simmer gently for about 10 minutes until vegetables are tender and fish flakes easily; if using frozen peas, add about 3 minutes before the end of cooking time. Strain off excess cooking liquid.

Meanwhile, in a small frying pan, heat oil, add remaining garlic and fry for 4-5 minutes until lightly coloured. Remove from heat and sprinkle in paprika. Stir quickly and pour over fish, potatoes and peas. Serve immediately.

Serves 4.

— COD WITH A PARSLEY CRUST —

750 g (1½ lb) cod, haddock or hake fillets, skinned
salt and freshly ground black pepper
2 cloves garlic, crushed
85 ml (3 fl oz/⅓ cup) olive oil
55 g (2 oz/1 cup) fresh breadcrumbs
2 tablespoons chopped fresh parsley
4 tablespoons lemon juice
parsley and lime wedges, to garnish

Season fish with salt and pepper and put in a shallow baking dish.

Mix together garlic and 4 tablespoons oil and pour over fish. Leave in a cool place for 1 hour. Preheat oven to 180C (350F/Gas 4).

Mix together breadcrumbs, parsley and lemon juice. Sprinkle evenly over fish, then trickle over remaining olive oil. Bake for about 15 minutes until fish flakes when tested with point of a sharp knife. Serve garnished with parsley and lime wedges.

Serves 4.

FISH IN GREEN SAUCE

3 tablespoons olive oil
4 hake or cod steaks, about 175 g (6 oz) each
½ Spanish onion, finely chopped
3 cloves garlic, chopped
115 ml (4 fl oz/½ cup) fish stock
2 tablespoons chopped fresh parsley
85 g (3 oz/¾ cup) slivered, roasted almonds
salt and freshly ground black pepper
dill sprigs, to garnish

Heat oil in a frying pan, add fish and cook for 2 minutes on each side.

Using a fish slice, transfer fish to a warmed plate, cover and keep warm. Add onion to oil remaining in pan and fry for 3 minutes. Stir in garlic and fry for 3 minutes, then stir in stock, parsley and almonds. Simmer for about 3 minutes until lightly thickened.

Transfer almond mixture to a blender or food processor and process until smooth. Season with salt and pepper. Return fish to pan, pour the sauce over the top and heat through for 1-2 minutes. Serve garnished with dill.

Serves 4.

COD & AUBERGINE

1 aubergine (eggplant), cubed
salt and freshly ground black pepper
750 g (1½ lb) thick cod fillet, cut into 4
150 g (5 oz) cured chorizo, skinned and thinly sliced
4 tablespoons olive oil
1 Spanish onion, finely chopped
2 cloves garlic, very finely chopped
1 red pepper (capsicum), peeled, seeded and cut into
   strips
450 g (1 lb) beefsteak tomatoes, peeled, seeded and
   chopped
115 ml (4 fl oz/½ cup) dry white wine
chopped fresh parsley, to garnish

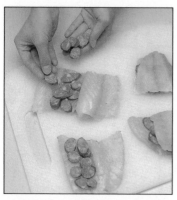

Place aubergine (eggplant) in a colander, sprinkle with salt and leave for 30 minutes. Rinse well and dry with absorbent kitchen paper. Halve each piece of cod horizontally without cutting completely in half. Open out like a book. Lay a quarter of the chorizo on one 'page' of each 'book', then cover with other 'page'. Heat oil in a flameproof casserole, add fish and cook until evenly browned. Using a fish slice, remove fish from casserole and set aside.

Add onion to casserole and cook slowly, for about 7 minutes, stirring occasionally, until soft but not coloured. Stir in garlic, aubergine (eggplant), and pepper (capsicum). Cook for about 4 minutes, then add tomatoes and wine and simmer for about 20 minutes until vegetables are tender. Season tomato mixture and return fish to casserole. Cook for a further 10 minutes. Garnish with parsley.

Serves 4.

—— SKATE WITH RED PEPPER ——

1 kg (2 lb) skate wings, skinned
salt and freshly ground black pepper
450 ml (16 fl oz/2 cups) dry white wine
225 ml (8 fl oz/1 cup) fish stock or water
2 tablespoons chopped Spanish onion
2 sprigs thyme
8 whole cloves
4 spring onions, thinly sliced
4 tablespoons mild red wine vinegar
2 tablespoons virgin olive oil
1 tablespoon lemon juice
1 red pepper (capsicum), thinly sliced
150 g (5 oz) French beans, halved diagonally
  lengthways

Rinse skate under cold running water, then season. In a large frying pan, bring wine, stock or water, onion, thyme and cloves to the boil. Lower heat, add skate and poach gently for about 12 minutes until flesh is opaque. Meanwhile, in a bowl, mix together spring onions, vinegar, olive oil and lemon juice. Set aside. Using a fish slice, transfer cooked skate to a warm plate and cover to keep warm.

Strain cooking liquid, then return it to pan. Add red pepper (capsicum) and salt and pepper. Simmer gently for 5 minutes. Add beans and cook for 5 minutes. Using a slotted spoon, transfer vegetables to a bowl. Boil liquid in pan for about 3 minutes until lightly syrupy, then pour into bowl with spring onion. Lift skate flesh from cartilage and place on a serving plate. Arrange vegetables around fish and spoon the spring onions and liquid over the top. Serve warm or cold.

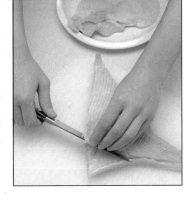

Serves 4.

ZARZUELA

16 mussels
350 g (12 oz) squid
3 tablespoons olive oil
450 g (1 lb) uncooked prawns in their shells
550 g (1¼ lb) monkfish, cut into 4 slices
salt and freshly ground black pepper
4 tablespoons Spanish brandy
1 large Spanish onion, finely chopped
1 teaspoon paprika
2 beefsteak tomatoes, peeled, seeded and chopped
1 bay leaf
115 ml (4 fl oz/½ cup) dry white wine
115 ml (4 fl oz/½ cup) fish stock
3 saffron threads, crushed
3 cloves garlic
3 tablespoons chopped fresh parsley

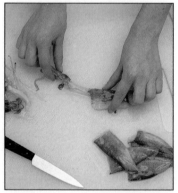

Clean and cook mussels (see page 12), remove from shells and set aside. Clean squid (see page 17), chop tentacles and slice bodies into rings; set aside.

Heat 3 tablespoons oil in a large flameproof casserole. Add prawns and fry until pink. Transfer to a plate. Season monkfish, add to oil and fry over medium heat until light brown. Add squid rings and tentacles and fry briefly. Pour in brandy, then set brandy alight. When flames die down, tip contents of casserole into a bowl and set aside.

Add onion to casserole and cook gently for about 4 minutes until soft. Stir in paprika and cook for 30-60 seconds.

Stir tomatoes into casserole with bay leaf and simmer for 2-3 minutes. Stir in wine and boil until reduced by a third. Stir in stock and simmer for 3-4 minutes.

Pound saffron, garlic and parsley together, mix in a little hot stock, then return to casserole. Boil for 1 minute. Add contents of bowl, the mussels and prawns and cook gently for about 5 minutes.

Serves 4.

——— BAKED SEA BREAM ———

2 sea bream, about 1 kg (2¼ lb) each, cleaned
salt and freshly ground black pepper
4 cloves garlic, crushed
2 sprigs parsley, chopped
4 tablespoons olive oil
juice 1 lemon
175 ml (6 fl oz/¾ cup) dry white wine
fennel and lemon slices, to garnish

Preheat oven to 190C (375F/Gas 5). Season fish inside and out with sea salt and black pepper.

Put in a shallow baking dish. Scatter garlic and parsley over fish. Pour over olive oil, lemon juice and wine.

Bake fish in the oven for about 20 minutes until flesh flakes easily. Serve garnished with fennel and lemon slices.

Serves 4.

──CHICKEN WITH PARSLEY──

3 tablespoons olive oil
1.75 kg (3½ lb) chicken, cut into 8 pieces
3 cloves garlic, lightly crushed
½ fresh red chilli, seeded and finely chopped
6 tablespoons dry white wine
salt and freshly ground black pepper
juice ½ lemon
3 tablespoons chopped fresh parsley

Heat oil in a flameproof casserole; add chicken and cook for about 10 minutes until lightly browned. Cook in batches, if necessary. Remove and reserve.

Add garlic and chilli to casserole and cook for 5 minutes without browning, stirring occasionally. Return chicken to casserole, pour the wine over it and allow to bubble for 2-3 minutes.

Season lightly, cover and cook gently for about 40 minutes until chicken juices run clear when pierced with a sharp knife. Transfer chicken to a warm plate and keep warm. Stir lemon juice and parsley into casserole. Boil if necessary to lightly concentrate juices, then pour it over the chicken.

Serves 4.

Variation: Use 4 large chicken portions, halved, instead of whole chicken.

- CHICKEN IN SANFAINA SAUCE -

4 tablespoons olive oil
1.5 kg (3 lb) chicken, cut into 8 pieces
2 Spanish onions, chopped
2 cloves garlic, chopped
1 green pepper (capsicum), seeded and sliced
1 red pepper (capsicum), seeded and sliced
2 aubergines (eggplants), cut into strips
115 g (4 oz) serrano ham, diced
450 g (1 lb) beefsteak tomatoes, peeled, seeded and
    chopped
115 ml (4 fl oz / ½ cup) dry white wine
115 ml (4 fl oz / ½ cup) chicken stock
bouquet garni of 1 bay leaf, 1 sprig thyme and 1 sprig
    parsley
salt and freshly ground black pepper
1 tablespoon chopped fresh parsley, to garnish

Heat oil in a large, heavy flameproof casserole, add chicken and fry until lightly
browned, about 10 minutes. Using a slotted
spoon, remove chicken and reserve. Add
onions and garlic to casserole and fry for
1 minute. Add peppers (capsicums) and
aubergines (eggplants) and cook, stirring
occasionally, for 5 minutes. Stir in ham,
tomatoes, wine, stock, bouquet garni and
salt and pepper.

Bring casserole to boil, then reduce heat so
liquid barely simmers. Return chicken to
casserole, bury it in sauce. Cover casserole
and cook gently for about 45 minutes until
chicken juices run clear when pierced with
sharp knife, and sauce is slightly thickened.
Discard bouquet garni. Taste and adjust the
seasoning. Serve sprinkled with parsley.

Serves 4.

Variation: Use 4 large chicken portions,
halved, instead of whole chicken.

CHICKEN WITH SHERRY

4 tablespoons raisins
225 ml (8 fl oz / 1 cup) oloroso sherry
3 tablespoons olive oil
1.75 kg (3½ lb) chicken, cut into 8 pieces (see page 66)
1 Spanish onion, finely chopped
1 clove garlic, finely chopped
225 ml (8 fl oz / 1 cup) chicken stock
salt and freshly ground black pepper
4 tablespoons pine nuts

In a small bowl, soak raisins in sherry for 30 minutes.

In a flameproof casserole, heat 2 tablespoons oil, add chicken and cook gently until lightly and evenly browned, about 10 minutes. Transfer to absorbent kitchen paper to drain. Add onion and garlic to casserole and cook gently, stirring occasionally, until softened and lightly coloured, about 7 minutes. Strain raisins and set aside.

Stir sherry into casserole. Simmer until reduced by half. Add stock, chicken and seasoning, bring to boil, then simmer gently until chicken is cooked, about 35 minutes. In a small pan, fry nuts in remaining oil until lightly coloured. Drain on absorbent kitchen paper, then stir into casserole with raisins. Transfer chicken to a warm serving dish. Boil liquid in casserole to concentrate slightly. Pour over chicken.

Serves 4.

SPICY CHICKEN

4 tablespoons olive oil
4 slices day-old French bread
8 cloves garlic
1.75 kg (3½ lb) chicken, skinned and cut into small
     pieces
300 ml (10 fl oz/1¼ cups) medium-bodied dry white
     wine
large pinch saffron threads, finely crushed
3 tablespoons chopped fresh parsley
3 cloves
freshly grated nutmeg
salt and freshly ground black pepper

Heat oil in a flameproof casserole, add bread and 5 garlic cloves and fry until browned.

Transfer to a mortar and crush, then transfer to a bowl. Crush remaining garlic and add to casserole with chicken. Cook until chicken changes colour. Pour in wine and just enough water to cover chicken. Cover casserole and simmer gently for about 30 minutes until chicken juices run clear when thickest part is pierced with a sharp knife.

Meanwhile, in a bowl dissolve saffron in 2 tablespoons of the chicken cooking liquid. Put parsley, cloves and nutmeg in the mortar and pound to a paste. Stir in the saffron. Mix with crushed bread, then stir the mixture into the casserole and cook for 10 minutes. Season to taste and serve.

Serves 4.

CHICKEN WITH WALNUT SAUCE

6 chicken breasts
salt and freshly ground black pepper
juice 1 orange
115 g (4 oz/1¼ cups) walnut halves
2 cloves garlic, chopped
85 ml (3 fl oz/⅓ cup) walnut oil
85 ml (3 fl oz/⅓ cup) olive oil
squeeze lemon juice
chopped fresh parsley or chives and lemon slices,
**   to garnish**

Preheat oven to 200C (400F/Gas 6). Season chicken breasts and pour the orange juice over them; set aside.

Spread walnuts on a baking sheet and place in oven until lightly browned, about 5-10 minutes. Transfer to a food processor or blender with garlic, 2 tablespoons water and a pinch of salt. Mix to a paste. With motor running, slowly pour in walnut and olive oils to make a smooth, mayonnaise-like sauce. Add lemon juice and pepper to taste; set aside.

Preheat grill. Grill chicken for 5-7 minutes each side until juices run clear when thickest part is pierced with a sharp knife. Garnish with chopped parsley or chives and lemon slices, then serve with the sauce.

Serves 6.

— CHICKEN IN VINEGAR SAUCE —

4 boneless chicken breasts, divided into fillets
salt and freshly ground black pepper
85 ml (3 fl oz/⅓ cup) olive oil
12 cloves garlic
1 small onion, finely chopped
about 3 tablespoons sherry vinegar
1 tablespoon paprika
1½ tablespoons chopped fresh oregano
2 tablespoons fresh breadcrumbs
300 ml (10 fl oz/1¼ cups) chicken stock
fresh herbs, to garnish

Season chicken with salt and pepper. Heat oil in a heavy flameproof casserole, add chicken and cook for 10 minutes.

Meanwhile, slice 4 of the garlic cloves. Add sliced garlic to casserole with the onion and cook until chicken is lightly browned all over, about 5 minutes more.

Remove chicken from casserole, stir in vinegar and boil for 2-3 minutes. Pound remaining garlic with a little salt, the paprika and oregano, then stir in breadcrumbs and a quarter of the stock. Pour over chicken, add remaining stock and cook for about 20 minutes until chicken is tender and sauce fairly thick. Adjust seasoning and amount of vinegar, if necessary. Serve garnished with fresh herbs.

Serves 4.

——————CHICKEN PEPITORIA——————

2 tablespoons olive oil
1.75 kg (3½ lb) chicken, cut into 8 pieces, or 4 large
  chicken portions, halved
½ Spanish onion, finely chopped
115 g (4 oz) serrano ham, cut into strips
225 ml (8 fl oz/1 cup) chicken stock
4 cloves garlic, crushed
20 g (¾ oz/15) almonds or hazelnuts, lightly roasted
pinch ground cloves
3 tablespoons chopped fresh parsley
3 egg yolks
salt and freshly ground black pepper

Heat oil in a flameproof casserole, add chicken and fry until lightly browned all over. Using a slotted spoon, remove chicken from casserole and set aside. Add onion to casserole and cook for about 4 minutes, stirring occasionally. Stir in ham, cook for 1 minute, then return chicken to casserole. Pour in the stock, cover tightly and simmer gently for about 45 minutes until chicken is tender.

Meanwhile, pound together garlic, nuts, cloves and parsley. Place in a small bowl and gradually work in egg yolks. Stir a little hot chicken liquid into the bowl, then stir mixture into the casserole. Continue to cook gently, stirring, until sauce thickens; do not allow to boil. Season with salt and pepper.

Serves 4.

—————CHICKEN & ALLIOLI—————

4 chicken portions
salt and freshly ground black pepper
6 tablespoons olive oil
3 tablespoons lemon juice
2 tablespoons finely chopped spring onions
2 tablespoons chopped fresh parsley
Allioli, see page 34
2 lemons, quartered

Rub chicken with salt and pepper, then place in a single layer in a non-metallic dish.

Pour the oil and lemon juice over the chicken and leave for 1 hour, turning chicken over once or twice.

Preheat grill. Place chicken on a grill rack and grill slowly for 8-10 minutes on each side, basting occasionally with the oil and lemon mixture, until crisp on the outside and tender throughout. Transfer to a warm serving plate and scatter spring onions and parsley over the top. Serve with Allioli and lemon quarters.

Serves 4.

QUAIL WITH GRAPES

3 tablespoons olive oil
1 Spanish onion, finely chopped
2 small carrots, finely chopped
salt and freshly ground black pepper
8 quail
8 slices streaky bacon
4 black peppercorns
2 cloves garlic
250 g (9 oz) moscatel grapes, peeled and seeded
pinch freshly grated nutmeg
225 ml (8 fl oz/1 cup) medium-bodied dry white wine
4 tablespoons Spanish brandy

Preheat oven to 190C (375F/Gas 5). Heat oil in a heavy flameproof casserole that will hold the quail in a single layer. Add onion and carrots and cook, stirring occasionally, for 4-5 minutes. Season quail inside and out, lay a slice of bacon over each one and tie in place with string. Place on the vegetables, then cook in the oven for 30 minutes.

Meanwhile, using a pestle and mortar, crush peppercorns and garlic, then work in half the grapes, the nutmeg, wine and brandy. Pour the mixture over the quail and cook for 30 minutes, basting occasionally. Add remaining grapes, then carefully pour cooking liquid into a saucepan; keep casserole warm. Boil liquid until lightly thickened, then season to taste. Transfer quail, bacon, vegetables and grapes to a warm serving plate and pour the sauce over them.

Serves 4-6.

SPANISH PARTRIDGE

2 partridges, halved along backbone
2 tablespoons brandy
salt and freshly ground black pepper
3 tablespoons olive oil
1 Spanish onion, chopped
3 cloves garlic, finely chopped
2 tablespoons plain flour
4 tablespoons red wine vinegar
225 ml (8 fl oz/1 cup) red wine
225 ml (8 fl oz/1 cup) chicken stock
6 black peppercorns
2 cloves
1 bay leaf
2 carrots, cut into short lengths
8 shallots
25 g (1 oz) plain (dark) chocolate, grated

Rub partridges with brandy, salt and pepper and set aside for 30 minutes. Heat oil in a heavy flameproof casserole into which the birds fit snugly. Add onion and fry, stirring occasionally, for 3 minutes. Stir in garlic and cook for 2 minutes.

Sprinkle birds lightly with flour, then fry in casserole for 5 minutes each side. Remove and set aside.

Stir vinegar into casserole and boil for 1-2 minutes. Add wine and boil for 1-2 minutes, then add stock, peppercorns, cloves, bay leaf and partridges. Heat to simmering point, cover tightly and cook gently for 40 minutes. Add carrots and shallots, cover again, and continue to cook gently for 20 minutes.

Transfer partridges, shallots and carrots to a warm dish. If necessary, boil the cooking juices until reduced to 300 ml (10 fl oz/ 1¼ cups), then purée in a blender or food processor.

Return juices to casserole, heat gently and stir in chocolate until melted. Return partridges and vegetables to casserole and turn them over in the sauce so they are well coated.

Serves 4.

──────DUCK WITH PEARS──────

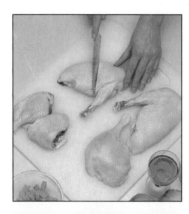

2 tablespoons olive oil
1 duck, cut into 8 serving pieces
2 Spanish onions, finely chopped
1 carrot, chopped
2 beefsteak tomatoes, peeled, seeded and chopped
1 cinnamon stick
1 teaspoon chopped fresh thyme
225 ml (8 fl oz/1 cup) chicken stock
4 tablespoons Spanish brandy
4 firm pears, peeled, cored and halved
1 clove garlic
10 almonds, toasted
salt and freshly ground black pepper
herbs, to garnish (optional)

Heat oil in a frying pan, add duck in batches, skin-side down, and cook over a fairly high heat for about 10 minutes until browned. Turn over and cook for about 8 minutes until underside is lightly browned. Using tongs, transfer duck to absorbent kitchen paper to drain.

Remove excess oil from pan, leaving about 2 tablespoons. Add onions, carrot, tomatoes, cinnamon and thyme and cook for about 5 minutes, stirring occasionally, until onions have softened but not browned. Add stock and simmer for 20 minutes.

Discard cinnamon and purée contents of pan in a food processor or blender, or rub through a sieve. Return this sauce to pan, add brandy and boil for 1-2 minutes. Add duck and heat through gently for 5-10 minutes.

Meanwhile, put pears in a saucepan into which they just fit. Just cover pears with water and simmer gently until tender.

Using a pestle and mortar, pound garlic and almonds to a paste. Mix in a little of the pear cooking liquid, then stir into sauce. Adjust consistency of sauce, if necessary, with more pear cooking liquid. Season to taste. Transfer duck to a warmed serving plate and pour the sauce over the top. Arrange pears around duck. Garnish with herbs, if desired.

Serves 4.

DUCK & OLIVES

3 tablespoons olive oil
2-2.5 kg (4-5 lb) duck, cut into 4 pieces
1 Spanish onion, finely chopped
1 tablespoon plain flour
2 beefsteak tomatoes, peeled, seeded and chopped
175 ml (6 fl oz/¾ cup) dry white wine
3 tablespoons water
4 bay leaves
3 sprigs parsley
3 cloves garlic, crushed
salt and freshly ground black pepper
225 g (8 oz) green olives

Heat half the oil in a heavy flameproof casserole. Add duck in batches, brown evenly, then transfer to absorbent kitchen paper to drain. Heat remaining oil in casserole, add onion and cook for 6-8 minutes, stirring occasionally, until golden and translucent. Stir in flour, then tomatoes, wine, water, bay leaves, parsley and garlic. Season with salt and pepper. Bring to boil, stirring. Add duck pieces, cover and cook gently for 30 minutes.

Put olives into a bowl, pour over boiling water, then drain well. Add to casserole, cover tightly and cook for about 30 minutes until juices run clear when thickest part of duck is pierced with a skewer. Skim excess fat from surface, and adjust seasoning, if necessary.

Serves 4.

LAMB CHILINDRON

4 tablespoons olive oil
750 g (1½ lb) lean lamb, cubed
salt and freshly ground black pepper
1 Spanish onion, chopped
2 cloves garlic, chopped
3 large red peppers (capsicums), peeled, seeded and
    cut into strips
4 beefsteak tomatoes, peeled, seeded and chopped
1 dried red chilli, chopped
chopped fresh herbs, to garnish

Heat oil in a flameproof casserole. Season
lamb and add to casserole.

Cook, stirring, until evenly browned, then
using a slotted spoon, transfer to a bowl. Add
onion to casserole and cook for about 4
minutes, stirring occasionally, until softened
but not coloured. Stir in garlic, cook for 1-2
minutes, then stir in peppers (capsicums),
tomatoes and chilli. Simmer for 5 minutes.

Return lamb, and any juices that have
collected in bowl, to casserole. Cover tightly
and cook gently for about 1½ hours until
lamb is tender. Season if necessary. Serve
garnished with chopped herbs.

Serves 6.

—LAMB WITH BLACK OLIVES—

4 tablespoons olive oil
750 g (1½ lb) lean lamb, cut into small cubes
115 g (4 oz) piece belly pork, cut into small strips
2 cloves garlic, sliced
½-1 teaspoon chopped fresh oregano
175 ml (6 fl oz/¾ cup) full-bodied white wine
1 fresh red chilli, seeded and finely chopped
12-15 black olives, stoned

Heat oil in a wide, shallow flameproof casserole. Add lamb, pork and garlic and cook over a high heat to seal and brown meat.

In a small saucepan, boil oregano and wine for 2-3 minutes. Stir into casserole, cover and cook gently for 30 minutes.

Stir chilli and olives into casserole. Cover again and cook for about 30 minutes until lamb is tender. If necessary, uncover casserole towards end of cooking time so liquid can evaporate to make a light sauce.

Serves 4.

—— SPICE-COATED LAMB ——

4 cloves garlic
¼ teaspoon cumin seeds
1 tablespoon paprika
¼ teaspoon saffron threads, crushed
salt and freshly ground black pepper
750 g (1½ lb) lean boned lamb, cut into 2.5-4 cm
    (1-1½ in) cubes
3 tablespoons olive oil
150 ml (5 fl oz/⅔ cup) full-bodied dry white wine

Using a pestle and mortar, pound together garlic, cumin, paprika, saffron, salt and pepper.

Put lamb into a bowl, add spice mixture and stir well but gently to coat lamb. Set aside for 30 minutes.

Heat oil in a flameproof casserole, add lamb and cook for 5-7 minutes, stirring occasionally, until lamb has browned. Stir in wine and heat to simmering point. Cover tightly and cook gently for about 30-40 minutes until meat is tender and sauce thickened.

Serves 4.

LAMB IN GREEN SAUCE

2 tablespoons olive oil
750 g (1½ lb) boneless lamb, cut into pieces
1 Spanish onion, chopped
2 green peppers (capsicums), seeded and chopped
3 cloves garlic, crushed
175 ml (6 fl oz/¾ cup) dry white wine
150 ml (5 fl oz/⅔ cup) water
1½ teaspoons chopped fresh thyme
salt and freshly ground black pepper
1 small round lettuce, sliced
2 tablespoons chopped fresh parsley
2 tablespoons chopped fresh mint
55 g (2 oz) pine nuts
mint sprigs and pine nuts, to garnish

In a flameproof casserole, heat oil, add lamb and fry, stirring occasionally, until evenly browned. Using a slotted spoon, remove lamb and set aside. Stir onion into casserole and cook for about 4 minutes, stirring occasionally, until softened but not browned. Stir in peppers (capsicums) and garlic, cook for 2-3 minutes, then stir in wine. Boil for 1 minute.

Pour in water and bring to the boil. Lower heat so liquid is just simmering, then add lamb, thyme and seasoning. Cover and cook gently for about 1 hour. Stir in lettuce, parsley, mint and pine nuts, cover and cook for a further 10-15 minutes. Serve garnished with sprigs of mint and pine nuts.

Serves 4.

– LAMB WITH LEMON & GARLIC –

3 tablespoons olive oil
1 kg (2¼ lb) lean, boneless lamb, cut into 2.5 cm (1 in) pieces
1 Spanish onion, finely chopped
3 cloves garlic, crushed
1 tablespoon paprika
3 tablespoons finely chopped fresh parsley
3 tablespoons lemon juice
salt and freshly ground black pepper
3 tablespoons dry white wine (optional)

Heat oil in a heavy flameproof casserole, add lamb and cook, stirring occasionally, until lightly browned. Do this in batches if necessary so the pieces are not crowded. Using a slotted spoon, transfer meat to a plate or bowl and reserve.

Stir onion into casserole and cook for about 5 minutes, stirring occasionally, until softened. Stir in garlic, cook for 2 minutes, then stir in paprika. When well blended, stir in lamb and any juices on plate or in bowl, the parsley, lemon juice and seasoning. Cover tightly and cook over very low heat for 1¼-1½ hours, shaking casserole occasionally, until lamb is very tender. If necessary, add wine or 3 tablespoons water.

Serves 4-6.

– BRAISED LAMB & VEGETABLES –

450 g (1 lb) firm, yellow-flesh potatoes, cut into 0.5 cm
 (¼ in) slices
2 cloves garlic, pounded to a paste
6-8 spring onions, thinly sliced
2 medium-large artichoke bottoms (see page 50), sliced
150 g (5 oz) chestnut mushrooms, chopped
handful parsley, finely chopped
1 tablespoon mixed herbs, chopped
salt and freshly ground black pepper
3 tablespoons olive oil
4 lamb shoulder or loin chops
175 ml (6 fl oz/¾ cup) full-bodied dry white wine

Preheat oven to 190C (375F/Gas 5). In a
bowl, combine potatoes, garlic, spring
onions, artichoke bottoms, mushrooms,
parsley, mixed herbs and seasoning. Place
half the mixture in a heavy flameproof
casserole. Heat oil in a frying pan, add lamb
and brown on both sides. Drain on absorbent
kitchen paper, then season and place in
casserole.

Over the heat, stir wine into pan to dislodge
cooking juices, bring to boil and pour over
lamb. Cover with remaining vegetables and
add sufficient water to come almost to the
level of the vegetables. Bring to the boil,
cover and cook in the oven for about 30
minutes. Uncover and cook for a further 1
hour. Add a little water if it seems to be
drying out.

Serves 4.

—— BEEF IN SPINACH SAUCE ——

2 tablespoons olive oil
750 g (1½ lb) chuck steak, cut into 4 cm (1½ in) cubes
8 button onions
1 tablespoon red wine vinegar
225 g (8 oz) fresh spinach, trimmed
1 tablespoon breadcrumbs
3 cloves garlic
425 ml (15 fl oz/scant 2 cups) veal stock, or water
salt and freshly ground black pepper
1 tablespoon black olive paste

In a large, flameproof casserole, heat oil, add beef and brown on all sides. Remove and set aside. Add onions to casserole and cook, stirring frequently, until evenly browned. Stir in vinegar and boil for 1 minute.

Put spinach, breadcrumbs, garlic and half the stock or water in a blender or food processor and mix until smooth. Return beef to casserole, pour over spinach mixture with remaining stock or water. Season. Heat to simmering point, then cover and simmer very gently for 1½-2 hours until beef is tender. Stir in black olive paste and serve.

Serves 4-6.

—BEEF WITH TOMATO SAUCE—

2 cloves garlic, thinly sliced
1 tablespoon finely chopped fresh thyme
1 tablespoon finely chopped fresh marjoram
750 g (1½ lb) piece chuck steak
2 tablespoons olive oil
SAUCE:
2 tablespoons olive oil
8 cloves garlic, chopped
1 sprig thyme
2 sprigs marjoram
3 sprigs parsley
400 g (14 oz) can chopped tomatoes
8 canned anchovy fillets, chopped
175 ml (6 fl oz/¾ cup) dry white wine
24 small black olives, stoned
salt and freshly ground black pepper

To make the sauce, heat oil in a saucepan, add garlic and herbs and cook gently for 5 minutes. Add tomatoes with their juice, then stir in anchovies, wine and olives. Simmer for 15 minutes. Taste and adjust seasoning.

Meanwhile, mix sliced garlic with chopped herbs. Using the point of a sharp knife, cut small slits in beef and push the herb-covered slices of garlic deep into slits. Heat oil in a flameproof casserole, add beef and cook until evenly browned, 10 minutes. Pour over sauce, cover tightly and cook gently for about 1½ hours turning beef occasionally, until it is tender.

Serves 4.

GARLIC BEEF

2 tablespoons olive oil
115 g (4 oz) piece green (unsmoked) bacon, cut into
   5 cm (2 in) cubes
1 kg (2 lb) chuck steak, cut into 4 cm (1½ in) cubes
1 Spanish onion, chopped
1 head garlic, divide into cloves
225 ml (8 fl oz/1 cup) red wine
2 cloves
bouquet garni of 1 sprig marjoram, 1 sprig thyme, 2
   sprigs parsley and 1 bay leaf
salt and freshly ground black pepper

In a heavy flameproof casserole, heat oil, add
bacon and cook over a low heat until bacon
gives off its fat. Increase heat, add beef and
cook for about 5 minutes, stirring occasionally, until browned all over. Using a slotted
spoon, transfer beef and bacon to a bowl.

Stir onion and garlic into casserole and cook
gently for 6 minutes, stirring occasionally.
Stir in wine, cloves, bouquet garni and salt
and pepper. Return meat to casserole, cover
tightly and cook gently for 2 hours, stirring
occasionally, until meat is very tender.
Check from time to time to ensure casserole is
not drying out.

Serves 6.

──PORK WITH HERB SAUCE──

25 g (1 oz/½ cup) fresh white breadcrumbs
2 tablespoons white wine vinegar
2 cloves garlic
2 canned anchovy fillets, drained
15 g (½ oz/¼ cup) chopped fresh parsley
2 teaspoons capers
1 hard-boiled egg yolk
225 ml (8 fl oz/1 cup) extra virgin olive oil
salt and freshly ground black pepper
4 loin chops, about 2.5 cm (1 in) thick

In a small bowl, soak the breadcrumbs in the white wine vinegar.

Meanwhile, using a pestle and mortar, crush garlic with anchovy fillets, parsley, capers and egg yolk. Squeeze vinegar from breadcrumbs, then mix breadcrumbs into mortar. Stir in oil in a slow trickle to make a creamy sauce. Add black pepper, and salt if necessary Set aside.

Preheat grill. Grill chops for about 12 minutes each side until lightly browned on both sides and cooked through but still juicy in centre. Season chops and spoon on some of sauce. Serve remaining sauce separately.

Serves 4.

—PORK IN CIDER & ORANGE—

3 tablespoons olive oil
flour for coating
salt and freshly ground black pepper
750 g (1 ½ lb) boned and rolled loin of pork
1 small Spanish onion, sliced
300 ml (10 fl oz/1 ¼ cups) well-flavoured dry cider
juice 1 large juicy orange
rind ¼ orange, cut into fine strips
pinch ground cinnamon
pinch caster sugar (optional)
thin orange slices, parsley sprigs and flaked toasted
    almonds, to garnish

Heat oil in a heavy flameproof casserole. Put flour on a plate and season with salt and pepper. Roll pork in seasoned flour to coat evenly and lightly. Add to casserole and brown evenly for about 10 minutes. Remove and keep warm. Stir onion into casserole and cook over a low heat for about 20 minutes, stirring occasionally, until very soft and lightly browned. Stir in cider, orange juice and rind strips and cinnamon. Bring to the boil and simmer for 2-3 minutes.

Return pork to casserole, turn it in sauce, cover and cook gently for about 45 minutes until pork is tender. Transfer pork to a serving dish and boil sauce, if necessary, to thicken lightly. Adjust seasoning and level of cinnamon, and add a pinch caster sugar, if desired. Pour sauce over pork and garnish with orange slices, parsley sprigs and toasted flaked almonds.

Serves 4.

SPICED PORK LOIN

1 tablespoon paprika
3 cloves garlic, finely crushed
1 teaspoon chopped fresh oregano
½ teaspoon finely crushed cumin seeds
1 bay leaf, crushed
salt
3 tablespoons virgin olive oil
750 g (1½ lb) boned and rolled loin of pork
olive oil for frying
4 tablespoons full-bodied dry white wine
stoned green olives, to serve

In a small bowl, mix together paprika, garlic, oregano, cumin seeds, bay leaf and salt, then stir in olive oil.

Place pork in a non-metallic dish, spoon the marinade mixture over the top, cover and leave in refrigerator for 2-3 days. Return pork to room temperature 30 minutes before cooking.

Cut pork into 4 slices. Heat oil in a frying pan over fairly high heat. Add pork, brown quickly on both sides, then cook more gently for 4-5 minutes a side until cooked through. Transfer slices to a warm serving plate. Stir wine into cooking juices, boil for 2-3 minutes, then pour over pork. Scatter green olives over the top.

Serves 4.

VEAL WITH ANCHOVIES

100 ml (3 ½ fl oz/scant ½ cup) olive oil
flour for coating
salt and freshly ground black pepper
4 veal loin chops, 2 cm (¾ in) thick
2 small cloves garlic, coarsely chopped
2 canned anchovy fillets, chopped
2 tablespoons chopped fresh parsley
1 ½ tablespoons coarsely chopped capers
squeeze lemon juice
parsley and lemon slices, to garnish

Heat 4 tablespoons oil in a frying pan large enough to take chops in a single layer. Season flour with salt and pepper, then dredge chops with seasoned flour.

Add chops to frying pan and cook for about 10 minutes, turning occasionally, until light brown and crisp on outside and just cooked in centre.

Meanwhile, in a small saucepan, heat remaining oil, add garlic and cook until garlic is pale gold. Stir in anchovies and parsley. Cook for 20-30 seconds, mashing and stirring anchovies with a wooden spoon. Add capers, and black pepper and lemon juice to taste. Transfer chops to a warmed plate and spoon the sauce over the top. Serve garnished with parsley and lemon slices.

Serves 4.

RICE & CHICKEN

3 tablespoons olive oil
1.4 kg (3 lb) chicken, cut into 8 pieces, or 4 large
  chicken pieces, halved
1 Spanish onion, finely chopped
2 cloves garlic, chopped
1 large red pepper (capsicum), cut into strips
1 tablespoon paprika
225 g (8 oz) beefsteak tomatoes, peeled, seeded and
  chopped
350 g (12 oz) risotto rice
¼ teaspoon saffron threads, finely crushed
850 ml (1½ pints/3¾ cups) boiling chicken stock, or
  water
150 g (5 oz) small shelled fresh or frozen peas
2 tablespoons chopped fresh parsley
lime wedges, to garnish

Heat oil in a paella pan or large frying pan.
Add chicken and cook for about 10 minutes
until a light golden colour all over. Remove
and set aside. Add onion, garlic and red
pepper (capsicum) to pan and cook gently for
8-10 minutes until vegetables are soft. Stir in
paprika, heat for about 30-60 seconds, then
add tomatoes and cook for about 10 minutes
until mixture is thick.

Add rice, stir for 2 minutes, then add saffron
and stock or water and quickly bring to the
boil. Return chicken to pan and simmer for
15 minutes. Add peas if using fresh ones and
continue to simmer for about 10 minutes
until chicken and rice are tender and most of
liquid has been absorbed. Add frozen peas, if
using. Remove from heat, cover pan and
leave for 5-10 minutes. Sprinkle with parsley.
Serve from pan if a paella pan has been used.

Serves 4.

PAELLA

4 tablespoons olive oil
1 kg (2 lb) chicken, cut into small pieces
2 Spanish onions, chopped
4 cloves garlic, chopped
1 tablespoon paprika
350 g (12 oz) risotto rice
3 beefsteak tomatoes, peeled, seeded and chopped
1.75 litres (3 pints/7½ cups) boiling chicken stock
1 sprig rosemary
salt and freshly ground black pepper
large pinch saffron threads, finely crushed
225 g (8 oz) small squid
150 g (5 oz) green beans
450 g (1 lb) mussels in their shells
225 g (8 oz) raw prawns in their shells
115 g (4 oz) broad beans

Heat oil in a 40 cm (16 in) paella or 4 litre (7 pint/18 cup) wide shallow casserole pan. Add chicken and cook for about 10 minutes until lightly browned. Add onions and garlic and fry for 5 minutes, then stir in paprika followed by rice. Stir for 2-3 minutes. Stir tomatoes into paella with stock, rosemary and salt and pepper. Dissolve saffron in 2 tablespoons stock, then add to paella. Boil for 8-10 minutes.

Prepare squid, see page 17; cut bodies into rings and chop tentacles. Cut green beans into short lengths. Scatter all seafood, green beans and broad beans into paella – do not stir. Gradually turn down heat and simmer for 8-10 minutes until rice is tender and liquid absorbed. Cover, remove from heat and leave for 5-10 minutes.

Serves 4.

Variation: Add 4 small rabbit portions with the chicken pieces.

FIDEUA

3-4 tablespoons olive oil
250 g (9 oz) raw Dublin Bay prawns
250 g (9 oz) raw prawns
salt
250 g (9 oz) monkfish fillet, cut into pieces
1 ½ teaspoons paprika
225 g (8 oz) beefsteak tomatoes, peeled, seeded and
   chopped
1.1 litres (2 ¼ pints/5 ½ cups) fish stock
2 cloves garlic
1 tablespoon chopped fresh parsley
6-8 saffron threads, finely crushed
250 g (9 oz) spaghettini, broken into lengths
lemon wedges and parsley sprigs, to garnish

Heat 3 tablespoons oil in a large paella pan or large frying pan, add Dublin Bay prawns, cook 1 minute then add prawns and sprinkle over a little salt. Fry shellfish on both sides for 2-3 minutes, then remove and set aside.

Add monkfish to pan and cook for a few minutes until lightly browned all over. Remove and set aside.

Add more oil to pan, if necessary. Stir in paprika, cook 30-60 seconds, then add tomatoes. Cook gently for about 5 minutes, stirring occasionally. Add stock and bring to the boil.

Pound garlic, parsley and saffron together. Stir in a little hot stock, then stir into pan and boil for 2 minutes. Add spaghettini and boil until pasta has absorbed most of the stock and is just tender.

Nestle monkfish and shellfish in the spaghettini, heat for 1-2 minutes, then remove from heat, cover pan and leave to stand for 5 minutes. Garnish with lemon wedges and parsley and serve from pan if a paella pan has been used.

Serves 4.

RICE & BLACK BEANS

2 tablespoons olive oil
1 Spanish onion, chopped
2 cloves garlic, chopped
115 g (4 oz) bacon, chopped
1 small red pepper (capsicum), chopped
1 teaspoon paprika
300 g (10 oz) beefsteak tomatoes, peeled, seeded and
    chopped
salt and freshly ground black pepper
225 g (8 oz) risotto rice
herb sprigs, to garnish
BEANS:
225 g (8 oz) black beans, soaked overnight and drained
½ Spanish onion
2 cloves garlic, crushed

To prepare the beans, put them in a saucepan with onion and garlic. Cover with plenty of water, bring to the boil, then simmer for 1½-2 hours until just tender. Meanwhile, in a saucepan, heat oil, add chopped onion, garlic, bacon and red pepper (capsicum) and cook, stirring occasionally, until bacon begins to brown. Stir in paprika for 30-60 seconds, then stir in tomatoes and cook for about 5 minutes, stirring occasionally. Season well.

Stir rice and 450 ml (16 fl oz/2 cups) water into pan with tomato mixture. Bring to the boil, stir, then simmer gently for about 25 minutes until liquid is absorbed and rice tender. Drain beans. Discard onion and garlic. Stir the beans into the rice mixture. Adjust seasoning and serve garnished with sprigs of herbs.

Serves 4-6.

——— SPICED RICE & PEPPERS ———

4 tablespoons olive oil
225 g (8 oz) long-grain rice
2 cloves garlic
salt
1 teaspoon each cumin and coriander seeds
3 tablespoons tomato purée (paste)
2 teaspoons paprika
1 teaspoon chilli powder
pinch saffron threads, crushed and dissolved in 2
    tablespoons boiling water
550 ml (20 fl oz/2½ cups) boiling chicken or vegetable
    stock or water
3-4 red peppers (capsicums), peeled, halved lengthways
    and seeded
extra virgin olive oil, to serve (optional)
chopped fresh herbs, to garnish

Heat oil in a paella pan or wide, heavy-based shallow saucepan. Stir in rice, then stir-fry for 2-3 minutes. Meanwhile, using a pestle and mortar, grind together garlic, salt, cumin and coriander seeds, then stir in tomato purée (paste), paprika, chilli and saffron liquid. Stir into rice. Stir in stock or water. Bring to boil, then cover and simmer for about 7 minutes.

Arrange peppers (capsicums) around sides of pan. Simmer for 7-10 minutes until rice is tender and plump, and liquid absorbed. Remove from heat and leave for 5 minutes. Trickle extra virgin oil over peppers (capsicums), if desired, and garnish with chopped herbs.

Serves 4.

——— RICE WITH CHICK PEAS ———

350 g (12 oz) chick peas, soaked overnight and drained
olive oil for frying
3 cloves garlic, finely chopped
225 g (8 oz) risotto rice
550 ml (20 fl oz/2½ cups) chicken stock, or water
1 quantity Tomato Sauce, see page 115
chopped fresh herbs, to garnish

Simmer chick peas in plenty of water for 1½-2 hours until just tender.

Meanwhile, prepare the rice. Heat 2 tablespoons oil in a saucepan, add garlic and fry for 2 minutes. Stir in rice, stir-fry for 3-4 minutes, then stir in 300 ml (10 fl oz/ 1¼ cups) stock or water. Simmer for 10 minutes, then add another 300 ml (10 fl oz/ 1¼ cups) stock or water. Continue cooking for 10-12 minutes until liquid is absorbed and rice tender. Cover and keep warm.

Drain chick peas. Heat about 1 cm (½ in) layer of oil in a frying pan, add chick peas and fry, stirring frequently, until golden brown. Stir into rice, then transfer to a warmed serving dish. Pour Tomato Sauce over chick peas and rice. Garnish with herbs and serve.

Serves 4.

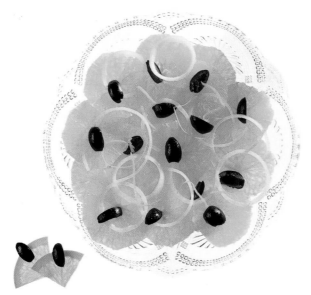

—VALENCIAN ORANGE SALAD—

4 large oranges
½ Spanish onion, thinly sliced
2 tablespoons white wine vinegar
85 ml (3 fl oz/⅓ cup) olive oil
salt and freshly ground black pepper
pinch caster sugar
stoned black olives, to garnish

Peel oranges and cut away pith and membrane from outsides. Thinly slice oranges and remove pips.

Push onion slices into rings. Arrange orange and onion slices on a plate.

In a small bowl, mix together vinegar, oil, salt and pepper and sugar. Pour dressing over the orange and onion slices. Scatter olives over the top, cover and chill in the refrigerator for 30 minutes before serving.

Serves 4-6.

──── ASPARAGUS WITH EGG ────

750 g (1½ lb) fresh asparagus
1 hard-boiled egg, finely chopped
85 ml (3 fl oz/⅓ cup) olive oil
1 clove garlic
45 g (1½ oz/¾ cup) fresh, coarse breadcrumbs
2 tablespoons chopped fresh parsley

Using a small sharp knife, cut off woody part at end of asparagus stems. Working from tip to base, scrape off scales from stems.

Tie stems into 4 bundles with tape or string. Bring 5 cm (2 in) level of water to the boil in a deep saucepan, add asparagus bundles, tips pointing upwards. Cover pan with a lid or dome of foil and simmer for 8-10 minutes until asparagus is just tender. Remove asparagus and untie bundles. Drain asparagus on a thick pad of absorbent kitchen paper. Arrange on a warm serving plate, sprinkle egg over stems, cover and keep warm.

Meanwhile, heat oil in a frying pan, add garlic and fry until lightly browned. Discard garlic. Stir breadcrumbs into pan and cook for 5-7 minutes, stirring, until crisp and golden. Remove from heat, stir in parsley, then pour it over the asparagus, leaving tips uncovered. Serve immediately.

Serves 4.

──── SPINACH WITH RAISINS ────

50 g (2 oz) raisins
1 kg (2 lb) spinach
3 tablespoons olive oil
1 clove garlic, finely chopped
3 tablespoons pine nuts
salt and freshly ground black pepper
croûtons, to serve

Put raisins into a small bowl, cover with boiling water and leave to soak.

Wash spinach, shake off surplus water but do not dry the leaves. Put into a large saucepan, cover and cook until spinach wilts. Uncover and cook until excess moisture has evaporated. Chop coarsely. Drain raisins.

Heat oil in a frying pan, add garlic and pine nuts and fry, stirring occasionally, until beginning to colour. Stir in spinach and raisins, add salt and pepper and cook over low heat for 5 minutes. Serve with croûtons sprinkled over the top.

Serves 4.

PISTO MANCHEGO

2 tablespoons olive oil
55 g (2 oz) bacon, chopped
2 large Spanish onions, chopped
1 clove garlic, chopped
2 courgettes (zucchini), chopped
4 red peppers (capsicums), peeled and chopped
450 g (1 lb) beefsteak tomatoes, peeled, seeded and
    chopped
bunch mint, parsley and basil, chopped
salt and freshly ground black pepper
4 poached or fried eggs, to serve (optional)

In a large frying pan, heat oil, add bacon, onions and garlic and cook gently for about 15 minutes, stirring occasionally, until onions are very soft and lightly coloured.

Add courgettes (zucchini) and peppers (capsicums) to pan and fry for about 4 minutes until soft. Stir in tomatoes and herbs and cook for 20-30 minutes until thickened. Season to taste. Serve topped by poached or fried eggs, if desired.

Serves 4.

—— BROAD BEANS WITH HAM ——

2 tablespoons olive oil
4 large spring onions, finely chopped
1 red pepper (capsicum), diced
55 g (2 oz) serrano ham, diced
450 g (1 lb) shelled broad beans
about 175 ml (6 fl oz/¾ cup) dry white wine
salt and freshly ground black pepper
chopped fresh herbs, to garnish (optional)

In a saucepan, heat oil, add spring onions, pepper (capsicum) and ham and cook for 3 minutes.

Stir in beans and cook for 1 minute. Add sufficient wine to cover, bring to boil, then cover pan and simmer gently for about 20 minutes until beans are tender.

Uncover and boil off excess liquid. Add black pepper, and salt, if necessary. Cool slightly before serving. Garnish with chopped herbs, if desired.

Serves 4.

—BAKED MIXED VEGETABLES—

450 g (1 lb) aubergines (eggplants), thinly sliced
salt and freshly ground black pepper
150 ml (5 fl oz/⅔ cup) olive oil
3 cloves garlic, crushed
450 g (1 lb) beefsteak tomatoes, peeled, seeded and
  chopped
1 tablespoon tomato purée (paste)
2 Spanish onions, thinly sliced
1 green pepper (capsicum), sliced
1 red pepper (capsicum), sliced
450 g (1 lb) potatoes, boiled and sliced
25 g (1 oz/½ cup) fresh breadcrumbs

Sprinkle aubergine (eggplant) slices with salt and leave in a colander for 30 minutes. Rinse under cold running water and dry well on absorbent kitchen paper. Meanwhile, in a saucepan, heat 1 tablespoon oil, add garlic and fry gently without browning. Add tomatoes, tomato purée (paste) and salt and pepper. Cover and simmer for 15 minutes. Preheat oven to 200C (400F/Gas 6). In a frying pan, heat 4 tablespoons oil.

Add onions and peppers (capsicums); cook gently for 15 minutes. Using a slotted spoon, remove from pan; set aside. Add remaining oil to pan. Add aubergine (eggplant) slices in batches; fry until golden. Drain on absorbent kitchen paper. Layer all the vegetables in a baking dish; season each layer and moisten with the tomato sauce. Finish with tomato sauce. Sprinkle with breadcrumbs. Bake for about 20 minutes until golden.

Serves 4-6.

——— HERBY PEAS ———

2 tablespoons olive oil
1 onion, finely chopped
2 cloves garlic, chopped
225 g (8 oz) shelled peas
115 ml (4 fl oz/½ cup) dry white wine
bouquet garni of 2 sprigs parsley, 1 sprig thyme and
   1 bay leaf
8 saffron threads
salt and freshly ground black pepper
mint sprigs and strips of peeled red pepper (capsicum),
   to garnish

In a flameproof casserole, heat oil, add onion and cook for about 5 minutes, stirring occasionally, until soft but not coloured. Add 1 clove garlic, cook for 1 minute, then stir in peas, wine and bouquet garni. Heat until simmering, then cover and cook gently for about 15 minutes until peas are tender. Discard bouquet garni.

Using a pestle and mortar, crush together remaining garlic, the saffron and a pinch salt to make a smooth paste. Stir in a little of the cooking liquid, then stir mixture into peas. Add black pepper and cook for a few more minutes. Serve garnished with mint sprigs and strips of red pepper (capsicum).

Serves 4.

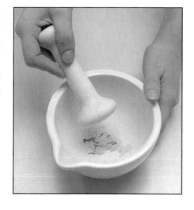

— POTATOES WITH CHORIZO —

4 tablespoons olive oil
115 g (4 oz) chorizo, chopped
750 g (1½ lb) potatoes, coarsely chopped
1 Spanish onion, chopped
1 red pepper (capsicum), chopped
350 g (12 oz) beefsteak tomatoes, peeled, seeded and
    chopped
salt and freshly ground black pepper
chicken or veal stock, or water, to cover
mint sprigs, to garnish

Heat oil in a flameproof casserole. Add
chorizo and cook, stirring occasionally, until
fat runs. Remove chorizo.

Add potatoes and onion and cook, stirring
occasionally, for 5 minutes. Stir in red pepper
(capsicum), fry for 5 minutes, then add
tomatoes and return chorizo to pan. Season
with salt and pepper.

Just cover with stock or water and simmer for
about 15 minutes until potatoes are tender
and most of the liquid has been absorbed.
Garnish with mint sprigs and serve.

Serves 4.

── BROCCOLI WITH CHILLIES ──

450 g (1 lb) broccoli
olive oil
2 cloves garlic, sliced
2 dried red chillies, seeded and crushed
salt

Cut thick broccoli stems in half or thirds lengthways. Add all of broccoli to a saucepan of boiling salted water, boil for 2 minutes, then drain and rinse under cold running water.

Heat olive oil in a heavy-based frying pan sufficiently large to hold broccoli in a single layer. Add garlic and chillies to pan. Cook over a moderate heat until sizzling, 3-4 minutes.

Add broccoli, turn to coat in oil then reduce heat to very low. Pour in 115 ml (4 fl oz/ ½ cup) water, add salt and cover tightly. Cook very gently for about 20 minutes, turning broccoli carefully 2 or 3 times, until broccoli is very tender. If necessary, uncover and boil off excess liquid. Serve hot or warm.

Serves 4.

CHURROS

olive oil for deep frying
mixture of vanilla caster sugar and icing sugar for
    dusting
Spanish Hot Chocolate, see page 117, to serve
DOUGH:
100 g (3½ oz/scant 1 cup) self-raising flour
¼ teaspoon ground cinnamon
55 g (2 oz/¼ cup) butter, diced
3-4 eggs, beaten

To make dough, sift flour and cinnamon onto a plate, or into a bowl, and place beside hob.

Gently heat butter in 175 ml (6 fl oz/¾ cup) water until butter has melted, then bring quickly to boil. Immediately remove from heat and quickly add flour mixture in one go and beat vigorously until smooth. Return to heat for about 30 seconds, still beating. Remove from heat and allow to cool slightly. Gradually beat in eggs until mixture is a smooth, thick glossy paste. Half fill a deep fat fryer or pan with oil and heat to 190C (375F).

Spoon dough into a piping bag fitted with a 0.5-1 cm (¼-½ in) plain nozzle and pipe 3 or 4 lengths into the hot oil, forming them into rings, spirals or horseshoes; use a sharp knife to cut off mixture at required length. Fry for about 3 minutes, turning once, until golden. Using a slotted spoon, transfer to absorbent kitchen paper to drain. Keep warm while frying remaining mixture. Dust thickly with sugar mixture and serve hot with Spanish Hot Chocolate.

Serves 4.

——OLIVE OIL & APPLE CAKE——

250 g (9 oz/2 cups plus 2 tablespoons) self-raising flour
¾ teaspoon ground cinnamon
85 g (3 oz/⅓ cup) caster sugar
finely grated rind and juice 1 lemon
2 eggs, beaten
3 tablespoons sweet sherry
160 ml (5½ fl oz/⅔ cup) olive oil
450 g (1 lb) crisp apples

Preheat oven to 180C (350F/Gas 4). Grease
an 18 cm (7 in) cake tin. In a bowl, stir
together flour, cinnamon, sugar and lemon
rind. Make a well in centre and gradually add
eggs, sherry, olive oil and lemon juice,
stirring to make a smooth mixture.

Peel, core and chop apples. Fold into cake
mixture and turn into prepared tin. Bake for
40-45 minutes until golden brown and firm to
the touch in centre. Leave for a few minutes
before turning onto a wire rack to cool.

Makes 8 slices.

LECHE FRITA

about 3 tablespoons caster sugar
3 eggs
55 g (2 oz/½ cup) plain flour
225 ml (8 fl oz/1 cup) whipping cream
225 ml (8 fl oz/1 cup) milk
few drops vanilla essence
100 g (3½ oz/1 cup) cake crumbs, preferably lemon
vegetable oil for deep frying

Lightly flour a baking sheet. In a bowl, beat together sugar and 2 eggs until pale. Gradually stir in flour.

In a heavy, preferably non-stick, saucepan, heat cream, milk and vanilla essence to boiling point. Slowly pour into the bowl, stirring. Return to heat and cook gently, stirring, until thickened; do not allow to boil. Pour onto baking sheet to make an even layer about 1 cm (½ in) thick, then leave to cool. Cover and refrigerate for at least 1 hour. Cut cold custard mixture into approximately 2.5 cm (1 in) squares rectangles or diamonds.

Beat remaining egg, then dip shapes first in beaten egg, then in the crumbs. Half fill a deep fat fryer or pan with vegetable oil and heat to 190C (375F). Add coated shapes in batches and cook for about 1½ minutes until golden and crisp on outside; keep an eye on temperature of the oil to make sure that it does not drop as the cubes should cook very quickly. Using a slotted spoon, transfer to absorbent kitchen paper, drain quickly and serve immediately.

Serves 4-6.

───── ORANGE 'FLAN' ─────

grated rind 1 orange
300 ml (10 fl oz/1¼ cups) fresh orange juice
3 whole eggs
3 egg yolks
2 tablespoons caster sugar
orange slices and mint, to decorate
CARAMEL:
115 g (4 oz/½ cup) caster sugar

Put orange rind and orange juice in a small bowl; set aside to soak. Preheat oven to 180C (350F/Gas 4). Warm 4 ramekin dishes.

To make the caramel, gently heat sugar in 1 tablespoon water in a small, heavy-based saucepan, swirling pan, until sugar has dissolved, then cook until golden brown. Immediately pour a quarter into each dish and swirl them around so caramel coats sides and base. Put in a baking tin. Gently heat orange juice and orange rind until just below simmering point.

Meanwhile, whisk whole eggs and egg yolks with sugar until thick, then slowly pour in orange juice and rind, whisking constantly. Divide between dishes then pour boiling water around them. Cover dishes with greaseproof paper then bake for about 25 minutes until lightly set. Remove dishes from baking tin and leave until cold. Just before serving, unmould puddings onto cold plates. Decorate with orange and mint.

Serves 4.

──SPANISH RICE PUDDING──

about 1.5 litres (2½ pints/6¼ cups) milk
1 cinnamon stick
2-3 strips lemon rind
pinch salt
70 g (2½ oz/⅓-½ cup) short-grain rice
70 g (2½ oz/¼-⅓ cup) caster sugar

Set aside 115 ml (4 fl oz/½ cup) milk. Heat remaining milk, cinnamon stick, lemon rind and salt to boiling point in a large saucepan. Stir in rice.

Lower heat so milk is only just simmering and cook for 15 minutes, stirring constantly, then leave to cook, uncovered, for about 1 hour, stirring occasionally. Stir in sugar.

Cook for a further 1 hour, stirring from time to time, until milk has been absorbed and pudding is very creamy and falls easily from spoon. Add some of reserved milk if mixture is too thick. Discard cinnamon stick and lemon rind. Serve hot, at room temperature or lightly chilled.

Serves 6.

Variation: Serve with fresh fruit and a sprinkling of cinnamon, if desired.

——————— BUNUELOS ———————

Churros dough, see page 108, made with 25 g (1 oz/6
    teaspoons) each butter and sugar, 5 tablespoons each
    milk and water, 55 g (2 oz/½ cup) self-raising flour,
    grated rind 1 lemon, 2½ eggs and 1 tablespoon
    Spanish brandy
olive oil for deep frying
2 tablespoons icing sugar
1 teaspoon ground cinnamon
FILLING:
85 g (3 oz/⅓ cup) caster sugar
85 g (3 oz/¾ cup) plain flour
2 eggs, beaten
500 ml (18 fl oz/2¼ cups) milk
grated rind 1 lemon
40 g (1½ oz/9 teaspoons) butter

To make filling, in a bowl, stir together sugar,
flour, eggs and a little milk. In a heavy,
preferably non-stick, saucepan, heat lemon
rind and remaining milk to boil. Slowly pour
into bowl, stirring. Return to pan. Heat
gently, stirring with a wooden spoon, until
sauce thickens; continue to heat gently for 5
minutes; do not allow to boil. Remove from
heat, stir in butter and cover closely with
greaseproof paper. Leave to cool.

Prepare dough, see page 108. Heat butter and
sugar in milk and water until butter has melted
and sugar dissolved. Add flour and lemon
rind, then beat in eggs and brandy. Heat oil in
a deep fat fryer to 180C (350F). Form dough
into small walnut-size balls and fry in batches
until evenly browned. Transfer to absorbent
kitchen paper while frying remaining mixture. Pierce a hole in the side of each ball and
fill with the filling. Serve hot dusted thickly
with the sugar mixed with the cinnamon.

Serves 4.

ROMESCO SAUCE

3 cloves garlic, unpeeled
225 g (8 oz) beefsteak tomatoes
1 red pepper (capsicum)
25 g (1 oz) blanched almonds, lightly toasted
1 dried hot red chilli, soaked in cold water for 30
    minutes, drained and seeded
3 tablespoons red wine vinegar
about 150 ml (5 fl oz/²⁄₃ cup) olive oil
salt

Preheat oven to its hottest setting. Bake garlic, tomatoes and red pepper (capsicum) for 20-30 minutes, removing tomatoes and garlic when soft and pepper (capsicum) when soft and lightly browned.

Peel tomatoes and pepper (capsicum) and discard seeds. Peel garlic. Mix vegetables with almonds and chilli in a blender or food processor, then, with the motor running, slowly pour in vinegar and enough oil to make a thick sauce.

Add salt to taste. Leave to stand for 3-4 hours before serving with meat, fish and vegetable dishes.

Serves 6.

Variation: True Romesco Sauce is made from romesco peppers (capsicums). If available, substitute 2 dried romesco peppers for the red pepper (capsicum) and chilli.

TOMATO SAUCE

2 tablespoons olive oil
½ Spanish onion, finely chopped
½ clove garlic, chopped
1 red pepper (capsicum), chopped
900 g (2 lb) beefsteak tomatoes, peeled, seeded and
  chopped
sugar or tomato purée (paste), (optional)
salt and freshly ground black pepper

Heat oil in a frying pan, add onion and cook
slowly for 5 minutes.

Stir in garlic and pepper (capsicum) and
continue to cook slowly for a further 10
minutes, stirring occasionally.

Stir tomatoes into pan. Simmer gently for 20-
30 minutes, stirring occasionally, until
thickened. Add sugar or tomato purée
(paste), if desired, and season with salt and
pepper. Mix in a blender or food processor, or
pass through a non-metallic sieve, if desired.

Serves 4-6.

— SPANISH COUNTRY BREAD —

225 g (8 oz/2 cups) strong flour
2 teaspoons salt, preferably coarse
3 teaspoons easy-blend dried yeast
oil for brushing
cornmeal for sprinkling

Sift flour and salt into a large bowl, stir in yeast and form a well in centre. Slowly pour 175 ml (6 fl oz/¾ cup) tepid water into well, stirring with a wooden spoon, to make a dough. Beat well until dough comes away from sides of bowl.

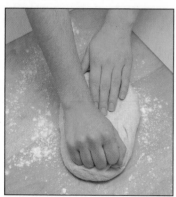

Turn dough onto a lightly floured surface and knead for 10-15 minutes until smooth and elastic; add a little more flour if dough is sticky. Put dough in an oiled bowl, cover and leave in a warm place until doubled in volume, about 2½ hours. Lightly sprinkle a baking sheet with cornmeal. Turn dough onto lightly floured surface, punch down then roll to a rectangle about 15 x 40 cm (6 x 16 in). Roll up like a Swiss roll and pinch seam to seal.

Place roll, seam-side down, on baking sheet. Using a very sharp knife, make 3 diagonal slashes on roll at equal distances. Brush top lightly with water. Leave in a warm place until doubled in volume, about 1 hour. Pre-heat oven to 230C (450F/Gas 8) and place a pan of water in the bottom. Brush loaf again with water and bake for 5 minutes. Remove pan of water. Brush loaf once more with water. Bake for about 20 minutes until loaf sounds hollow underneath.

Makes 1 loaf.

—SPANISH HOT CHOCOLATE—

85 g (3 oz) plain (dark) chocolate, broken into pieces
450 ml (16 fl oz/2 cups) milk
cinnamon sticks and orange rind, to decorate

Put chocolate in top of a double boiler or a bowl placed over a saucepan of hot water. Leave chocolate to melt.

Heat milk to boiling point. Using a wooden spoon, slowly stir a little boiling milk into chocolate.

Using a wire whisk, whisk in remaining milk and continue to whisk until mixture is frothy. Pour into heatproof glasses or cups and decorate with cinnamon sticks and orange rind.

Serves 2.

Variation: Rub 2 sugar cubes over a whole orange to extract the zest, then add the sugar to the hot milk. Sprinkle cinnamon on the top of the hot chocolate.

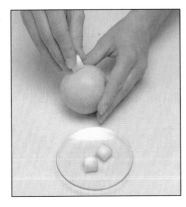

HORCHTA

225 g (8 oz) tiger nuts
1 litre (1 ¾ pints/4 ½ cups) water
finely grated rind ½ lemon
about 85 g (3 oz/⅓ cup) sugar

Rinse nuts well under cold running water.
Soak in clean water overnight. Drain.

In a blender or food processor, process nuts
with sufficient of the water to make a fine
paste. Return mixture to the bowl and add
remaining water, lemon rind and sugar
to taste.

Leave in a cold place for 4 hours. Strain the
liquid through a muslin-lined sieve. Chill
until ice cold.

Serves 4.

Note: Some of the horchta can be poured
into a metal tray and frozen until slushy, then
add to the drink as it is served.

SANGRIA

6-8 ice cubes
1 bottle red wine, chilled
2 strips orange peel
2 strips lemon peel
juice 4 oranges
2 tablespoons caster sugar
juice 2 lemons
685 ml (24 fl oz/3 cups) soda water, chilled
mint sprigs and orange and lemon slices

Put ice cubes in a large cold bowl, pour in the wine and add strips orange and lemon peel.

Put orange juice in a small bowl, add sugar and stir until sugar dissolves. Stir into wine with lemon juice. Top up with soda water. Pour into a large, cold serving jug. Decorate with mint sprigs and orange and lemon slices.

Serves 4.

INDEX